HUMAN SERVICE STRIKES

A Contemporary Ethical Dilemma

Eugene Lauer

WITHDRAWN

The Catholic Health Association
OF THE UNITED STATES

Library of Congress Cataloging-in-Publication Data

Lauer, Eugene F., 1935-
    Human service strikes.

    Includes index.
        1. Strikes and lockouts—United States. 2. Strikes and lockouts—United States—Religious aspects—Christianity. 3. Strikes and lockouts—United States—Moral and ethical aspects. I. Title. [DNLM: 1. Ethics. 2. Strikes, Employee. HD 5324 L372h]
HD5324.L34   1986   331.89′281′000973   86-6848
ISBN 0-87125-113-2

"...dreaming of systems so perfect,
no one will need to be good."
—Mohandas Gandhi

Contents

Preface

When strikes by human service workers became common in the United States in the 1960s, many of us probably experienced ambivalent feelings. On the one hand, we felt a certain bond with the workers. Teachers, nurses, police, firefighters, and other human service employees had traditionally been paid much less than workers in profit-making industries. Society had generally treated them in a patronizing fashion, applauding their fine motivation but considering them to be outside the "real world" of business and politics.

We have a proud tradition of being *"for* the working person" in the United States, of being on the side of the "underdog." Thus many Americans had a natural tendency to support the new assertiveness of workers in the helping professions. It seemed right and just that they should gain more control over their economic situation and have more power to shape the policies that governed them in the delivery of their services.

On the other hand, many of us had uneasy feelings about a teacher refusing to teach students because of a salary dispute with a local school board. We hesitated before completely supporting a nurse who withdrew care from patients until a new fringe benefit package had been negotiated.

The source of this uneasiness was clear. Different from most profit-making enterprises, a third party, the client, was caught in the middle to these conflicts.[1] Often the clients had personal relationships with the human service workers. In many cases the clients were people who had little power in our society: the aged, the poor, the very young, and the physically or mentally handicapped. The clients, who were neither responsible for the dispute nor capable of resolving it, often seemed to suffer the most until the strike was settled.

How can we resolve these ambivalent feelings? Reflection on this question leads us into the moral/ethical realm. Many people seemed to be saying, "It's just *not right*" for the nurses, police, teachers, and firefighters to withdraw their services from the people who need them. The public, consciously or unconsciously, was making a moral/ethical judgment about the right of human service workers to strike. By examining the moral/ethical dimensions of this issue, I believe that we can take a step forward in resolving the ambivalence just described. Such a resolution is a primary goal of this work.

As I began research on this topic, I quickly discovered that little had been written on the moral/ethical dimensions of human service strikes. Moral theology and social ethics textbooks have only brief references to human service strikes in them, usually general, rather negative comments. Many articles in professional journals comment on this subject, but most are written from an advocacy point of view, often defending or condemning a specific strike. Few, if any, are careful evaluations of the moral/ethical principles involved in striking.

Many authors have written about the legal dimensions of such strikes in law journals and anthologies. Although this point of view is not specifically that of a professional ethicist or moral theologian, it does attempt to answer the questions, "Is it *right* for service workers to strike? Is this *correct* behavior?" Even though asked in terms of legal considerations, these questions necessarily touch on some of the moral/ethical issues of striking. Thus I found many arguments in such articles to be valuable in formulating a moral/ethical position.

The only book I discovered on the morality of striking (primarily about industrial strikes, since it was written before human service strikes became common) was Donald A. McLean's *The Morality of the Strike* (New York, P.J. Kenedy & Sons), written in 1921! The information and line of argumentation were obviously dated, but the book proved quite valuable for tracing how moral/ethical thinking in striking has evolved since the first quarter of this century.

The "revisionist approach"[2] to contemporary theology guided me to research this book in a somewhat nontraditional way. Revisionist theologians maintain that human experience is a genuine *source* for theology and not simply an aid to our understanding of theology. (A more developed explanation of the role of experience in theological process appears in Chapter One.) We can unfold the meaning of Christian Scripture, traditionally considered to be *the* source for Christian theology, only if we have had some experience of the realities that the words in revelation connote. The experiences themselves are part of theology's basic content and of the "revelation from the divine" in the human condition.

It would have been unthinkable, therefore, to proceed to research a topic like human service strikes without listening to and probing the experiences of people who have been involved in labor-management relations, collective bargaining, and the strike experience. The labor leaders (local, national, international), management personnel, superintendents and presidents of institutions, mediators and arbiters, teachers, nurses, police, public service workers, and others whom I interviewed were all very willing to share their experiences with me. Perhaps they were unaware that we were "doing theology/ethics" as we conversed, but they were indeed "theologizing" in the best sense of the word as they relived their experiences with me.

I did not conduct these interviews according to the scientific methodologies of the social sciences. I was not seeking a valid sampling of opinions that would give sufficient data for sociological conclusions. I was not doing psychological case studies from which I could construct an empirical theory.

As a theologian, I was testing ideas that I had read or that I had thought out in the "crucible of experience," which philosopher Martin D'Arcy calls "the best of all crucibles." Experience simply "does not allow a gross lie to have a long life; it challenges it with constant contradictions."[3] I was attempting to discover if anything in these ideas was grounded in reality. It is of little value to speculate about an hypothesis if the hypothesis has almost no chance of ever being realized. For example, to argue that nurses' strikes would be immoral if patients had no one to care for them as they came out of emergency surgery is useless speculation when one discovers that such a situation almost never happens in a nurses' strike. The primary purpose of the interviews was to ensure that the hypotheses, speculations, and principles in this book would be based on what actually has happened, is happening, and probably will continue to happen in human service strikes.

As I progressed in doing the interviews, I discovered that in many cases it was helpful for the sake of complete openness to assure people that I would not quote them directly. Thus I have made it a general rule in writing this book to quote only written sources directly. I will make general references, however, to the interviews regularly throughout the volume.

In writing, I have a bias toward brevity. In this complex modern age, we are literally inundated with oceans of words from every imaginable medium. An old German proverb, "Allzuviel ist ungesund," reminds us that too much, even of a good thing, is unhealthful. For the sake of a brevity that heightens clarity, I am limiting the scope of this book to the single topic of the morality of the human service strike itself: *What can we say about the rightness or wrongness of human service workers withholding their services from clients in order to put pressure on management in the collective bargaining process?*

Striking when a no-strike law exists, violating court injunctions, using intimidation and violence on either side during a job action, etc., are all important moral/ethical issues. They are intimately related to our central topic, but I will not treat them directly in this book, in the interest of presenting, as clearly and undistractedly as possible, an analysis of *the foundational issue.*

Up to this point I have used the combined term, "moral/ethical," and the double nouns, "moral theology and ethics," when I wished to refer to the question the rightness or wrongness of an action. I have done so because I take the position that no essential difference exists between ethics and moral theology.[4] (I explain this contemporary theory of how the two disciplines are identified in Chapter One.) For simplicity of expression, I will henceforth use either "moral" or "ethical" and "moral theology" or "ethics" without any essential distinction of meaning.

I am indebted to many people for their suggestions and their insights which helped to shape this book. I wish to thank the hundreds of interesting people—too numerous to mention by name—who shared their experiences, their feelings, their convictions and their wonderments with me in formal interviews and in informal conversations. However, I would be remiss if I did not mention at least some of the people who made special contributions to the shaping of this study.

Thomas Donahue, Secretary-Treasurer of the AFL-CIO, John Sweeney, President of the Service Employees International Union, and Robert Kliesmet, President of the International Union of Police Associations, generously shared with me their experiences of long years of union activity and of painful involvement in many strikes. I am particularly grateful to Gerald Shea, Healthcare Industry Coordinator of the Service Employees International Union, not only for a fascinating interview, but also for arranging interviews with several other very helpful people and for leading me to a wealth of printed sources on my topic.

William Abelow, President and Counsel for the League of Voluntary Hospitals & Homes of New York, contributed a host of new insights about the thinking of management concerning human service strikes, insights sharpened by his experience of the New York Hospital Strike of 1984. Rosemary Donley, Dean of the School of Nursing (and soon to be Academic Vice-President) at The Catholic University of America, shared reflections with me from both management and workers' points of view, and arranged a score of interviews with management personnel and nurses who had been involved in hospital strikes.

Nurses Connie Dennis and Glennda Harrison made me very aware that human beings do not live by ideas alone with their detailed descriptions of their feelings during the Washington Hospital Center strike of 1978, as well as those of their striking and nonstriking colleagues. Albert Fondy, President of the American Federation of Teachers Local in Pittsburgh and veteran of a number of strikes, provided some very challenging perceptions about the complex position of teachers during strikes. R. H. Trivus, former superintendent of Mayview State Hospital in Pittsburgh, was equally challenging in describing the role of management personnel during a strike at an institution for people with mental illnesses. Harold Hirsh, a doctor, lawyer, and educator, contributed a multifaceted view of the problem of striking from his involvement in labor relations in many different roles.

I owe a special word of thanks to Diana Vahabzadeh, a graduate assistant at Duquesne University in the 1970s, who aided me in arranging the first interviews and in pursuing my initial bibliographical research on the topic.

From two of my colleagues at The Catholic University of America, I learned the ideal way to do research. The ideal way to do research is to ask some scholar-friends at dinner about some sources, and then wake up the next morning to find the sources outside one's door. I am deeply indebted to Charles E. Curran and Robert Friday, moral theologians in the School of Religious Studies at The Catholic University of America, for graciously teaching me this wonderful research method. I am grateful, too, for their careful reading of sections of the manuscript and for their many expert suggestions.

Ellen Rufft, a former member of the English faculty at LaRoche College in Pittsburgh (and now a counseling psychologist), read the entire manuscript with an eye for style, word-usage and clarity that would be the envy of any copy editor on the continent. I am most grateful to her for the scores of suggestions that she made that have helped to make this book more readable. I am indebted to her also for guiding me to some excellent sources on the psychology of power and assertiveness.

Finally, I owe a great debt of thanks to Msgr. George Higgins, Professorial Lecturer at The Catholic University of America, who introduced me to the national and international labor-relations scene "in the twinkling of an eye." His willingness to share his prodigious expertise, gained through forty years of rubbing shoulders with most of the great labor leaders in the western world, and his guiding me to interviews with many of those leaders, were invaluable resources for such a project. As the beneficiary of his wisdom and experience, it is easy for me to understand the following quotation from the renowned American Church historian, John Tracy Ellis: "More than once I have said that, all things considered, I regard Monsignor Higgins as the best informed Catholic priest in the United States."

Once again, I express my gratitude to the hundreds of other union and management personnel, theologians, nursing faculty, economists, and labor relations experts, students and friends whose ideas, impressions, and feelings have profoundly influenced the shaping of theories in this volume.

Notes

1. I will use the term "client" consistently throughout the book to designate anyone who is the recipient of a directly delivered human service. Although the term does not always fit our common use of language for human services (e.g., those who receive education are called "students," those who receive hospital care are called "patients"), it will be convenient to have a single term for all the recipients of the great variety of human services.

2. David Tracy, *Blessed Rage for Order* (New York: Seabury Press, 1975), pp. 32-34.

3. Martin D'Arcy, *The Mind and Heart of Love, Lion and Unicorn: A Study in Eros and Agape* (New York: Henry Holt & Co., 1947), p. 156.

4. See Charles E. Curran and Richard A. McCormick, eds., *Readings in Moral Theology No. 2: The Distinctiveness of Christian Ethics* (New York: Paulist Press, 1980).

Part I

Background of the Issue

Chapter 1

A "Theology" of
Human Service Strikes?

Can there be such a thing as a "Christian theology" of human service strikes? Certainly Jesus never gave any exhortations to the Pharisees, Scribes, or his apostles about when to withhold their services. If Christian faith and theology are scripturally based, then how can we speak of a genuine Christian theology of a phenomenon that has arisen (at least on a major scale) only in the second half of the twentieth century?

The answer lies in the fact that Christian theology is not simply an unfolding of the meaning of Scripture. It is much more than simply trying to find Scripture passages that might apply to modern problems. According to contemporary theologians, Christian theology is more accurately described as the process of thinking about issues from a Christian perspective. It is a pondering of modern problems from a point of view that is immersed in and shaped by Jesus' teachings.

Hans Küng maintains that a Christian is one who is so attached to the *person* of Jesus Christ that he or she makes decisions based primarily on that relationship. "The special feature, the most fundamental characteristic of Christianity is that it considers this Jesus as ultimately decisive, definitive, *archetypal* for human beings"[1] — in all their judgments, in everything they do. If they enter deeply into their relationship with Jesus Christ, Christians believe that they will have a special ability to see the divine dimension within human experience.

Thus, even though Christian Scripture records only a few passing remarks about the relationships between laborers and their masters in the first century, there can be nonetheless an authentic Christian theology of labor relations. When Christians become absorbed in their relationship with Jesus and attempt to live out his teachings in their daily work and their relations with their employees and employers, they are capable of shaping a theory of their experiences based on the divine reflection inside all human reality.

Role of human experience in theology

A group of contemporary theologians known as the "revisionists"[2] place much more emphasis on the role of human experience in shaping Christian theology than did traditional theologians. The revisionists maintain that the words of revelation (found essentially in the Scriptures) can have no meaning unless they address realities that are already part of our consciousness and have already been part of our experience. "Instead of using only revelation and tradition as starting points, as classical theology has generally done, it [theology] must start with facts and questions derived from the world and from history."[3]

Jesus' command to "love everyone" can have little or no meaning to people who have never experienced love or who have not struggled to love people they did not find particularly appealing. People who have loved others and been loved in many different kinds of relationships will immediately resonate with this command. When Jesus speaks, they will hear not just his words but their own experiences echoing within them.

Human experience is, therefore, not simply an *aid* to fashioning Christian theology. It is a genuine *source* of Christian theology, because much of theology's content comes from the lived experiences of human beings.[4]

To evaluate people's experiences accurately, one should not simply ask such questions as, "What do you think about this?" or "What do you think is right?" When people are asked what "they think" about an issue, they will most often fashion an opinion about how life *should be* and how people *ought to* act. It is far more fundamental and valuable for theological reflection to discover people's perceptions of what it was like to live through the experience. Therefore, to get to the raw material for Christian theology, one should ask, "What was your experience like?" and "How did you relate to others as you went through it?"

What are some of the "lived experiences" that we must reflect on to fashion a moral theology of human service strikes? We must reflect on and evaluate the frustrations of human service workers, so often in an inferior role in our society. We must understand the ambivalence they feel as they strain for justice for themselves and their clients in a system that has frequently patronized them but not authentically respected them. We must analyze the powerlessness that clients and the general public often feel when certain human services are not available during a strike. We must ponder the inner struggles of management personnel who have come into their positions primarily because of an authentic interest in the delivery of human services. We must try to get to the root of the ambivalence that many people feel when such strikes occur.

To come to some resolution of the problem of strikes, the theologian cannot simply advocate the just demands of any one group involved. The theologian must bring traditional Christian values into the reflective process on all the experiences just listed, confident that a resolution can be found in the midst of conflicting needs and demands. Some Christian moral values that seem most applicable to the question of human service strikes—and that are often sources of conflict—are the following: authentic self-love; the sharing of power; the risk of harm to clients; and the question of people's rights to health care, education, and public safety. A discussion of these values is the primary focus of Part II of this book.

Every Christian believer "does theology." We cannot help but do it if we are interested in the meaning of right and wrong and how to live in a Christian way in the modern world. As people try to express "the meaning of their inner experience of faith, they are involved in the theological enterprise....The difference between the ordinary member of the Church and the theologian, is then a difference in degree and not in kind. It is a matter of scientific sophistication and not of fundamentally different tasks."[5] In this volume I am attempting to put into a more sophisticated and systematic form the theology taking shape in the minds of those who have lived through human service strikes.

A major problem is present in an approach to theology that places such heavy emphasis on human experience. If many people's experiences of the same event are so different and in conflict, will it not be impossible to draw any conclusions about what is right or wrong in the experience? Does not an experientialist approach to moral decision making allow each individual person's experience to become decisive in judging the personal morality of an event?

Such total open-endedness is not the necessary conclusion to an experientialist approach. Christian revelation teaches that God made human beings in "the image and likeness of God" and that something divine resides in us all, forming a divine common denominator. Even though individuals may apparently experience an event like a human service strike in different ways, Christian revelation gives us confidence that we will be able to find, at some level of our experience, common human instincts and senses of direction that stem from our common divine reflection. Perhaps we may never be able to articulate these common denominators perfectly, but we can give some expression to them sufficient to guide us in the direction of goodness and truth.[6]

In using an experiential approach to moral theology, any one of us can easily fall into the trap of relying too heavily *on one experience* and wanting to make that experience the norm for everyone, especially when a single experience has been very deep and moving. Such a narrow reliance on a single experience can become a prejudice rather than an insight. Charles E. Curran cautions us well: "Sometimes experience of only one side of a question will definitely prejudice my understanding of the total human situation with which I am confronted."[7] In evaluating the morality of human service strikes, we must be particularly sensitive to this caution, since many clients, workers, and management personnel have deep-seated emotional ties to their roles in delivery of human services and can easily conclude that the only authentic way to view a strike is from their own perspective.

In this contemporary revisionist approach, we see that the definition of moral theology has changed somewhat. Previous definitions emphasized that moral theology was a study of Christian principles and revelation as applied to human acts to determine their rightness or wrongness. A simple modern definition has a different tone: "[Moral theology is] the reflective systematic study of Christian life and action."[8] The raw material studied is not exclusively Christian principles and biblical concepts. The lives and actions of people of all cultures as they struggle, grow, and change in their efforts to live out Christ's example are the main focus for the contemporary theologian's study of morality.

A specifically Christian ethic?

If such a thing as a Christian ethic for human service strikes exists, should it apply only to Christians? Many contemporary moral theologians give an interesting analysis of the relationship between Christian ethics and a natural human ethics that is valuable for answering this question.

The most basic observation we can make about this issue is that "the God of revelation is also the God who created this human world."[9] God did not reveal to human beings a pattern of behavior that contradicts the inner directions that the Divine Source put inside human beings at creation. For Christians, God can certainly be mysterious but not inconsistent.

What can be distinctively Christian is the *approach* to ethical issues. Christian theologians presume that the person and actions of Jesus are normative for human behavior.[10] To discover the depths of Jesus' being and the fundamental rationale for his actions is to discover the fullness of being human. Jesus never leads us away from authentic human development.

Thus, Christian theology approaches moral issues with distinctive presuppositions. Christian theologians, however, are confident that any well-disposed human being could come to the same moral conclusions as Christians by examining human experience and the divine reflection within all persons and events.[11]

An accurate moral conclusion about human service strikes, if carefully worked out from an understanding of human experience and Christian teaching, states something universal about human behavior and does not simply give us a "Christian rule." Christian faith presupposes and Christian Scriptures claim that "the Christian self-understanding does, in fact, express an understanding of authentic human existence as such...."[12]

How could one prove this claim? There can be no way to prove it absolutely through logic or empirical data, although these may have some persuasive power. One must appeal ultimately to the inner experience of the reader or listener and ask, "Does this moral conclusion resonate with your experience? Does it fit the instinctive directions that you find deep within yourself?" I propose these two questions to every reader as he or she evaluates the moral analysis of human service strikes in this volume.

Changes in moral thinking: an historical context

Why are such dramatic changes occurring in the approach to moral decision making among Christian theologians and ethicists today? A brief survey of the historical development of Christian moral thinking provides valuable insights for understanding these changing patterns of thought and specific clues to understanding how to develop a moral theology of human service strikes.

In any area of investigation, what is happening at present is best understood in the light of how it developed originally. We can grasp any concept or direction of thought more confidently if we are aware of the past influences and events that shaped the idea in its present form. We gain little by studying an "idea in itself"; such things do not exist. "Everything is the sum of the past," wrote Teilhard de Chardin. "Nothing is comprehensible except through its history."[13]

How did Christian theology, particularly moral theology, develop into its present form? And—especially interesting for our specific study— *who* were those most responsible for that development? Figure 1 divides the history of Christian theology into four periods.[14] In 1965 a new age of theology begins, especially in the Catholic tradition, with the conclusion of the Second Vatican Council.

Figure 1.

Historical Development of Christian Theology

Patristic age	Dark ages	Scholastic age	Post-Reformation
AD ca. 600	ca. 1100	ca. 1500	1965
•	•	•	•

Bishops	Monks	University Professors	Seminary Professors

What did the major theologians of each age of theological development have in common? *Who* and *what* were the bishops, monks, university professors, and seminary professors? First, they were all *men*; almost no women have been moral or doctrinal theologians in Christianity until the contemporary period. Second, almost all have been *ordained clergy*; very few have been laity.

Third, most theologians have been *white* males from the First and Second World, Europe, and North America; few have been people of color from the Third World. Finally, until the Protestant Reformation, almost all these men were *celibate* (except for certain small groups in the patristic period). Most theologians in the Protestant tradition, of course, have been married.

According to Karl Rahner, Christianity is a universal religion, not just in its missionary hope that it should be preached to all people, but because its teachings can and must be shaped by all peoples of all cultures.[15] In the light of this historical outline, Christian moral and doctrinal theology clearly has had a very narrow development. A small, select, and homogeneous group of people have shaped it.

Who is missing from theological development? Four groups have not been involved in the process: women, laity, people of color, and during most periods married persons. In other words, the experiences of *most Christian believers* have not been involved in the process of shaping Christian moral and doctrinal teaching.

Two insights from this historical analysis are immediately valuable in shaping a moral theology of human service strikes. The first concerns women. As the feminist movement has demonstrated, women have been an oppressed group in every period of history and in almost every culture.[16] Also, most human service workers have traditionally been women, especially in the areas of health care, education, and child care.

Women were also socialized to think that they should never be concerned about their own needs. "The work that woman does...is felt to have value only insofar as it frees others to participate in the public world. But this means that woman understands her own worth only in terms of what she can do for others and is therefore...dependent on others for her own self-definition."[17] Women have been socialized to feel guilty about even an authentic concern for self.

This manipulative socialization of women became somewhat normative for all persons working in human services. "How dare you ever think about yourself!" has been the challenge to anyone involved in delivering human services. An atmosphere is created wherein it becomes sinfully selfish for human service workers to care about their own needs when they are serving clients who need something from them. In the past two decades, women have entered into the theological enterprise with a new assertiveness and have helped to expose the fallacy of such a position. Shaping a moral position on human service strikes is influenced significantly by this new awareness that the identity of women should not and must not come solely from their relationships to persons they serve.

The second insight from the historical analysis is an expansion of the first. Of the four groups traditionally excluded from theological development, two are always included by social scientists and theologians among "the oppressed": women and people of color, especially those from the Third World. Three "new technologies" in the Christian tradition come from the experience of these two groups: black theology, liberation theology, and feminist theology.

Besides a woman's perspective expanding the vision of Christian theology, similar new realizations come from black and liberation theology that will also affect this discussion of human service workers and their strikes. For example, is black theologian James Cone accurate when he observes that those who are accustomed to having authority *can never be trusted* to safeguard the interests of those who are subject to them and that those with authority must *be forced* to share it?[18] Is liberation theologian Gustavo Gutierrez correct when he insists that no one is poor or oppressed by accident and that people are *made* poor or oppressed by unjust systems that need to be challenged and reformed?[19] Such strong assertions can cast Christian moral thinking in a radically different mold.

Contemporary Christian moral thinking cannot afford to ignore this flood of new insights from sources once untapped, especially when dealing with an issue like labor-management relations in human services. Problems in this area constantly involve power struggles between authority figures and workers, challenges to systems that make and keep people poor, and so on.

Possibility of absolute ethical answers

Another dimension of Christian moral theology has been undergoing significant reconsideration in the last three decades: the question of absolutes. Can human beings in their faith tradition declare certain actions to be always right and others to be always wrong? From the revisionist point of view, I will first give a blunt answer and then a fuller explanation. Can absolutes exist? Yes, but as limited human beings we will probably never know them completely nor be able to articulate them perfectly. In practical terms, therefore, we will never have absolutes for solving every situation that arises.

The rationale for this statement follows. God is perfect and absolute. We believe that the perfect god has entered the human condition and spoken to us. Although God can communicate the divine absoluteness to us, we are incapable of receiving the divine message perfectly.[20] We are imperfect, limited human beings who have been further weakened by the universal sinfulness of the human condition. We are incapable of "taking in" the final divine truth once and for all. We will never be able to express it fully and unambiguously.

Thus a function of Christian moral theology is to refine continually the understanding of the divine directions that we have through faith. We pursue the divine absoluteness and approach it more closely, but we never capture it completely. A review of the way in which the Christian tradition has developed a moral position on the taking of a human life will make this theoretical explanation more concrete.

At one stage in Christian development, Christian teachers said that God's commandment was clear: human beings were not to kill other human beings. Only God has control over life. Then Christians reflected on their experience more deeply and decided that God meant that human beings should not kill innocent people. When aggressive people attacked innocent people, either individually or at war, no choice remained but to kill the aggressors lest they kill the innocent.

Later in the Christian tradition, when life experiences became more complex, some Christian teachers decided that sometimes it was necessary—and thereby moral—to take innocent life indirectly, e.g., when bombing an enemy munitions plant located in a residential section of a city or in removing a cancerous uterus when a woman was pregnant. Some theologians today have challenged the value of this distinction between direct and indirect, expecially when they found cases in which exactly the same results occurred whether the taking of life was direct or indirect.[21] Thus the absolute principle went from not killing human beings to a sometimes challenged and difficult-to-determine position of not directly killing innocent human beings.

Revisionists point out how absolutely certain some Christian teachers were, at each developmental stage, that their view was the final view, the exact understanding of divine revelation. Each time a succeeding group of teachers revised the view and showed how it was either incomplete or inaccurate. Many revisionists therefore would maintain that all we can say conclusively about a theology of the value of human life is that the Christian tradition has great respect for human life because it is God-given, that innocent human beings deserve greater protection than aggressive persons, and that a Christian enters any moral judgement with a bias in favor of life.

Thus some contemporary theologians are very cautious about "absolutizing any present structures, institutions, or ideals"[22] (e.g., "unions are absolutely necessary for all classes of workers to obtain justice"; "strikes against charitable institutions can never be justified"). The Christian community has discovered that some of the principles or structures of thought that were absolutized in the past turned out to be very limited and historically conditioned realities.

When searching for divine truth, one can easily fall into the trap of presuming that certain appealing and logical ideas or patterns of behavior must have divine approval. When they are attractive, reasonable, and workable, "existing social arrangements or structures could very easily be mistaken for the eternally willed order of God."[23]

A central theme from biblical theology provides another basis to moral theologians for determining if absolutes can exist in moral theology: the coming of the "reign of God."[24] This biblical term does not connote an empire, nor the establishment of some sort of spiritual nation. It means rather that God so touches the human spirit that people accept the power of God as the only and ultimate power in their lives. If people live within the reign of God, then the final criterion for deciding what human activity is proper is the divine presence, the divine will.

The application of this theme to moral absolutes is simple. If the reign of God is present now in the limited human condition, then Christ's commands are absolute and apply to everyone equally. We must absolutely love all human beings, no matter how obnoxious they may be. We must never use violence but always turn the other cheek. We must never divorce and remarry, no matter what the circumstances. We must forgive perfectly and endlessly, despite what people do to us. To act otherwise is to sin.

If the reign of God is still to come, however, then Christ's commands are ideals to strive for, not commands to be absolutely obeyed. We must do our best to love everyone, to avoid violence, and to remain faithful in marriage, but we are as yet incapable of living perfectly and acting ideally. To make some exceptions to these ideals is imperfection, not sin. We await Christ's Second Coming when the reign of God will be perfected in us. Only then will we be capable of living out the ideals of Christ perfectly.

How do most biblical theologians answer this question about the coming of the reign of God? Practical people who desire clear and direct answers will be disappointed with their reply. Most scholars conclude that the "seeds of the reign of God" have been planted with the coming of Christ, but these seeds will not come to full fruition until the Second Coming.[25] Their answer is in-between.

This in-between answer, however, leads to the conclusion that moral absolutes can be with us only in the period of the perfect coming of the reign of God. Until then we strive for the divine ideals, knowing that as limited human beings we are incapable of achieving them fully.

Charles E. Curran describes the imperfect state of the human condition from another point of view that is particularly helpful in attempting to understand the dynamic of human service strikes. In the human condition, some conflict is inevitable; living in perfect harmony with everyone is impossible. From a theological point of view, Curran speaks of four sources of conflict.[26]

The first source is the most obvious: we are limited, finite creatures. By God's intent in creation, we are not "finished products." We are imperfect creatures striving to be better. Limited creatures cannot help but disagree on how to strive for their ideals.

Second, according to our traditional teaching of original sin, all people born into the world are further weakened by sin. In contemporary theology, original sin is neither a stain on the soul nor some sort of genetic defect passed on from parents to children. Rather, it is the state of the world. Original sin is "the continually perpetuated perversion of humankind, in which new sins are conditioned more or less by the preceding sins and carry on the existing disorder....Each of us, because we are born into a world and a race contaminated by sin, is born a sinner."[27] A disordered, sinful world will inevitably be a source of conflict for us all.

Third, conflicts arise because of different subjective approaches to the same object; e.g., in a strike one person shouts, "I am pressuring an unjust employer," and another retorts, "You are hurting an innocent client." Finally, conflicts arise because God has communicated divine truth to us but we cannot grasp it firmly. We have a taste of the divine, but we yearn for the day when we can absorb God fully—the day of the Second Coming.

It is not unusual and is even expected that people of good will with the finest intentions will come into conflict. A religious group opens a nursing home with the pure intention of serving the poor and the aged. They hire equally well-intentioned professionals and support staff. How could any serious confrontation possibly occur? Their differences are rarely caused by ill will, at least not initially. The differences arise because they are all limited, sinful, subjective human beings as they struggle for their ultimate ideals.

Consequently, we begin our inquiry into the moral dimensions of human service strikes knowing that we are unable to arrive at such conclusions as, "Physicians strikes are always unethical" or "There is never any moral problem with teachers' strikes." Rather, our conclusions will tend to delineate under what conditions and in what circumstances such strikes may be moral or immoral.

In the "heat of battle," i.e., in formulating adversary positions in tense experiences during strikes, it is interesting (and understandable, given human emotions) to discover how absolute and all-encompassing advocates on either side can be about their ethical conclusions. (I say this not as a criticism but as a caution. Our finest moral judgments rarely come in the most heated moments of conflict.)

Amid the great tension of the 1919 Boston police strike, Calvin Coolidge pronounced with greater infallibility than the pope: "There is no right to strike against the public safety by anybody, anywhere, anytime."[28] President Franklin D. Roosevelt called public service strikes against the government "unthinkable and intolerable."[29] The noted Catholic moral theologian Bernard Haring concluded that "strikes that deprive people of important public services...should *absolutely* be avoided."[30]

On the other hand, union advocates have been equally absolute in declaring that, "There is not, never has been, and never will be any substitute for the right of employees to withhold their labor as a method of advancing their interests."[31] Another author asserts with finality that "no employer . . . can be trusted to exercise power without restraint and checks and counterbalancing influences on the exercise of authority . . . . Economic and personal security . . . can be achieved *only* through effective human organization."[32]

Sound moral judgment is rarely so absolute.

"Relational" model for moral decision making

Moral theologians like Charles E. Curran, Richard McCormick, and Daniel McGuire draw together these more open-ended approaches to moral decision making in a system that Curran names the relationality-responsibility model."[33] According to this model, all the actions and events of human life are more accurately defined in terms of relationships rather than in terms of substances, at least when applied to moral decision making. For example, anger is best defined by judging how it affects family networks, spousal relationships, etc., rather than by judging it bad or good on the basis of its intensity. A heart transplant is best understood in terms of how persons can and should relate to one another rather than in terms of its technical biochemical procedures and how these fit the passive laws of nature.

This model maintains that all life actions and events can be understood through four relationships: to God, to other people, to the physical world, and to self.[34] Moral decision making should always account for how an act changes or disrupts or enhances these four relationships. The person making the decision should be confronted with the responsibility for maintaining and enhancing these four relationships—thus a *relationality* and *responsibility* model.

Moral theologian Daniel Maguire gives a simple description of this approach to moral decision making that encompasses both its experiential and its relational dimensions. The foundations of morality are not merely biblical prescriptions; along with the sources of revelation, "the foundation of morality is the experience of the value of persons and their environment. . . . Ethics exists as an effort to see what does and does not befit persons in all of their marvelous and compelling valuableness and sacredness."[35]

What I have found fascinating in my research about this relationality-responsibility model is that the theologians who propose it do not overtly connect it to another area of research that is moving in an almost identical path, psychological research into the different ways in which men and women make their moral decisions.

Carol Gilligan began this research at Harvard University. She discoverd that men traditionally make their moral judgments based on clear-cut rules and principles. Generally, it seems right and just to men to follow these rules, no matter how difficult the situation, as long as everyone is aware of them beforehand.

Whereas men think more in terms of strict justice, women think more about specific persons.[36] Consequently, women tend to make moral judgments more relationally: how will everyone involved be affected by the moral decision? The common thread here is "the wish not to hurt others and the hope that in morality lies a way of solving conflicts so that no one will be hurt."[37] Something in women's decision-making process guides them to presume that no rules could possibly have foreseen all future variations and circumstances of human actions; therefore, no rules could possibly be applied without exception to all situations.

Whether women and men have been socialized to think in these patterns or whether something innate is present in each sex that causes such directions of thought is not the focus of Dr. Gilligan's research. She is simply presenting the facts that have emerged, without attempting to draw a conclusion about their origins.

The observations made in this book about human service strikes do not depend on the exact source of these sexual differences. What is significant is that the experiences of women have been different from those of men and that male experience almost exclusively has been the raw material for shaping Christian morality. Perhaps the relationality-responsibility model has taken into account, consciously or unconsciously, the experiences of women much more than traditional Christian morality. This discussion of human service strikes must continue to do so, since the experiences of women form a major portion of the raw material to be analyzed.

Summary: toward a theology of human service strikes

In this opening chapter I have attempted to point out those facets of contemporary theology that are of special significance for fashioning a moral theology of human service strikes. These facets do not make up the *content* of a moral theology of strikes; rather they describe the *approach* to that theology.

First, the experiences of everyone involved in a human service strike must be investigated in order to fashion a realistic theology: the strikers, nonstrikers, clients, management personnel, and general public. To emphasize the experience of one group only leads to shaping an advocacy position, not a reflective ethic.

Second, we presume that a Christian ethic and a human ethic are the same. The approach of a Christian theologian and a humanistic ethicist may be different, but the raw material of human experience they analyze is the same. Any sound conclusions should find some resonance and affirmation within the hearts and experiences of most people of good will.

Third, a theology that comes from the Christian tradition of the 1980s must not be inspired and developed solely from the reflections of white, male, celibate (in the Catholic tradition) clergy. The experiential reflections, especially of women and minorities, are crucial to shaping an informed theology of human service strikes because of the various ways in which those two groups are involved.

Fourth, in fashioning conclusions about the morality of human service strikes, the reasoning in this book follows the contemporary nonabsolutist approach. Absolutes, if they do exist, will never be captured perfectly and articulated adequately by us finite creatures. As good human beings and as faithful Christians, we strive to know and to practice ultimate ideals but patiently recognize our limitations in attaining them, intellectually and in our actions.

Finally, human relationships are the basic stuff of which human reality is made. Human relationships are at least as important as wages, job titles, and the mending of broken bones. Considering education, health, etc., simply as measurable, concrete commodities is not an accurate analysis of human affairs. To some degree they are, but this is only a partial view. Health care, education, and public safety are *frameworks for relationships*, relationships that give our lives their basic meaning. A contemporary moral theology of human service strikes must recognize the fundamental value of, and give primary consideration to, the relationships that constitute the very fiber of our existence.

Notes

1. Hans Küng, *On Being a Christian* (New York: Doubleday Publishing Co., 1976), p. 123.

2. For a brief description of the revisionist school of thought, see David Tracy, *Blessed Rage for Order* (New York: Seabury Press, 1975), pp. 32-34.

3. Yves Congar, *Situation et taches presentes de la theologie* (Paris: Les Editions du Cerf, 1967), p. 72.

4. Tracy, pp. 43-44.

5. Timothy E. O'Connell, *Principles for a Christian Morality* (New York: Seabury Press, 1976), p. 5.

6. Anthony Battaglia, *Towards A Reformulation of Natural Law* (New York: Seabury Press, 1981), pp. 15-16; see Tracy, p. 44.

7. Charles E. Curran, *New Perspectives in Moral Theology* (Notre Dame, IN: Fides Publishing Co., 1974), p. 15.

8. Charles E. Curran, *Transition and Tradition in Moral Theology* (Notre Dame, IN: University of Notre Dame Press, 1979), p. 15.

9. O'Connell, pp. 6-7.

10. Küng, pp. 123-126.

11. Charles E. Curran, "Is There A Catholic/Christian Ethic?" in Charles E. Curran and Richard A. McCormick, eds., *Readings in Moral Theology No. 2: The Distinctiveness of Christian Ethics* (New York: Paulist Press, 1980), p. 77 and throughout; see also Charles E. Curran, *Catholic Moral Theology in Dialogue* (Notre Dame, IN: Fides Publishing Co., 1972), pp. 16-21.

12. Tracy, p. 44.

13. Teilhard de Chardin, *The Future of Man* (New York: Harper & Row, Publishers, Inc., 1964), p. 12.

14. This chart is derived from the analyses of the development of Christian theology in Paul Tillich, *A History of Christian Thought* (New York: Harper & Row Publishers, Inc., 1968); Bernhard Lohse, *A Short History of Christian Doctrine* (Philadelphia: Fortress Press, 1966); T.A. Burkill, *The Evolution of Christian Thought* (Ithaca, NY: Cornell University Press, 1971); and Hans Kung, *The Council, Reform and Reunion* (New York: Sheed & Ward, 1962).

15. Karl Rahner, "Towards a Fundamental Theological Interpretation of Vatican II," an address at an academic convocation of the Weston School of Theology, Cambridge, MA, April 8, 1979; trans. by Leo J. O'Donovan.

16. Mary Daly, *Gyn/Econogy* (Boston: Beacon Press, 1978), pp. 1-105.

17. Judith Plaskow, *Sex, Sin and Grace* (Washington, DC: University Press of America, 1980), p. 14. See also Madonna Kolbenschlag, *Kiss Sleeping Beauty Good-Bye* (New York: Bantam Books, 1979), p. 9.

18. James Cone, *Black Theology and Black Power* (New York: Seabury Press, 1969), p. 12.

19. Gustavo Gutierrez, *A Theology of Liberation* (Maryknoll, NY: Orbis Books, 1973), pp. 292-295.

20. John Henry Newman, *An Essay on the Development of Christian Doctrine* (New York: Image Books, 1960), p. 53. Newman was one of the first Christian scholars to understand and give expression to the theory that the unfolding of Christian revelation is a never-ending process and that human beings will never fully capture divine meaning.

21. Charles E. Curran, *Themes in Fundamental Moral Theology* (Notre Dame, IN: University of Notre Dame Press, 1977), pp. 124-125.

22. Curran, p. 78.

23. Curran, p. 78.

24. Rudolf Schnackenburg, *The Moral Teaching of the New Testament* (New York: Scabury Press, 1973), p. 13.

25. Hans Küng, *The Church* (New York: Sheed & Ward, 1967), pp. 56-57.

26. Curran, pp. 357-359.

27. A.M. Dubarle, *The Biblical Doctrine of Original Sin* (New York: Herder & Herder, 1964), pp. 224-225.

28. "The Right to Strike," in R.E. Walsh, ed., *Sorry...No Government Today* (Boston: Beacon Press, 1969), p. 235.

29. David L. Colton and Edith E. Graber, *Enjoining Teacher Strikes* (St. Louis: Center for the Study of Law in Education, Washington University, 1980), p. 9.

30. Bernard Haring, *Free and Faithful in Christ*, vol. 3 (New York: Crossroad Publishing Co., 1981), p. 301.

31. Murray B. Nesbitt, *Labor Relations in the Federal Government Service* (Washington, DC: Bureau of National Affairs, Inc., 1976), p. 375.

32. Jack Barbash, *Union Philosophy and the Professional* (unpublished paper for the Department of Labor Studies, Pennsylvania State University, 1978), pp. 3, 5.

33. Charles E. Curran, "Utilitarianism and Contemporary Moral Theology: Situating the Debate, in Charles E. Curran and Richard A. McCormick, eds., *Readings in Moral Theology No. 1: Moral Norms and Catholic Tradition* (New York: Paulist Press, 1979), p. 356.

34. Curran, *Transitions and Traditions...*, p. 22; Curran, "Utilitarianism...," p. 356; Eugene F. Lauer and Joel Mlecko, eds., *A Christian Understanding of the Human Person* (New York: Paulist Press, 1982),

pp. 1-5; Charles E. Curran, "The Person as Moral Agent and Subject in the Light of Contemporary Christology," in Francis A. Eigo, ed., *Called to Love: Towards a Contemporary Christian Ethic* (Villanova, PA: Villanova University Press, 1985), pp. 31-32.

35. Daniel C. Maguire, *The Moral Choice* (Garden City, NY: Doubleday Publishing Co., 1978), pp. 72-73.

36. Carol Gilligan, *In A Different Voice* (Cambridge, MA: Harvard University Press, 1982), pp. 62-63.

37. Gilligan, p. 65.

Chapter 2

Nature and Evolution of Strikes

Following the assertions made in Chapter One about theological method and human experience, this chapter begins the discussion of a moral theology of human service strikes with a look at history, not with an analysis of theories. How did workers decide to stop working in order to pressure their employers? What motivated them? What did they intend to accomplish by such action?

We best understand any phenomenon by trying to discover how it developed to its present form. As mentioned, no such thing as an "idea in itself" exists. Every concept and theory exists in a context that has a history. By digging into that history, we discover the experiences that are the theory's foundation, and those experiences lead us to ultimate meaning much more quickly and accurately than speculation about ideas.

Even a cursory look at the historical development of strikes reveals that they did not evolve through careful planning and testing. Strikes happened, then people theorized about them. As in most human activities, workers responded *instinctively* to what they perceived to be great injustices inflicted on them. They confronted those in authority by refusing to do what the authority figures wanted from them. They refused to work. As history unfolds, theorists analyze the various tactics and pressures involved in this instinctive reaction and develop them into well-planned strategies.

A study of the history of strikes also reveals how much they belong to the nineteenth and twentieth centuries, even though as far back as the third millenium BC, work stoppages by laborers and craftspersons took place during the building of the great pyramid of Cheops in Egypt. In the first millenium BC, Roman slaves and gladiators revolted and Greek silver miners rebelled at Laurium.[1]

Medieval historians record work stoppages in the fourteenth century by valets and shearmen, girdle makers, and tanners.[2]

Such work stoppages, however, were rare and dramatic occurrences, indeed minor rebellions before the modern period. Only with the Industrial Revolution did strikes become part of the regular flow of life for workers. I am not suggesting, by using the phrase "regular flow of life," that strikes quickly became accepted procedures comparable to taking a few days sick leave. Such an interpretation would not be true even today. Rather, the possibility of a strike became a factor that everyone regularly had to consider in labor-management relations when serious conflict occurred. Strikes became "part of the game" in the nineteenth and twentieth centuries.

The fact that striking became an established methodology during the Industrial Revolution suggests a conclusion that I propose now and argue for throughout the book. Striking belongs more to a capitalist mass production system of labor-management relations than it does to worker-employer relations in general. The phenomenon of striking does not necessarily come from one person being the employer and the other the worker, as some theorists suggest today. It stems more specifically from the way the employer-worker system is arranged. The historical facts seem to confirm this assertion, as I attempt to demonstrate in the following pages.

I make this suggestion here to challenge a certain trend of thinking, discussed in Chapter Three, that presupposes that striking is a "natural phenomenon." I am proposing that this position is an overstatement. Striking may be more accurately described as a creation of human beings devised to deal with the difficulties involved in labor-management relations, especially in a specific economic system like mass production capitalism.

Finally, by reviewing the history of striking, one discovers that the term "strike" does not have one easily articulated meaning. The common denominator present in every use of the term is work stoppage. In motivation, goals, and manner of execution, however, the term has many meanings. Some strikes are *protests*; others are *demonstrations*. According to another theory, every strike is a minirevolution. Most often today, a strike is a pressure tactic workers use in the collective bargaining process and is referred to technically as a direct strike.

This review and analysis of the different kinds of strikes that developed in history provide a valuable context for viewing the exact nature of a human service strike. Human service strikes evolved only after industrial strikes had been refined for over a century. Human service strikes are most often direct strikes but sometimes have a certain flavor of demonstration and protest about them.

Earliest developments

The little information available gives some indication of the motivation for those "job actions" already mentioned. The Roman slaves and gladiators, the Greek silver miners, and the Egyptian pyramid builders felt powerless in their situations. They worked extraordinarily long hours and instinctively felt a need for some freedom in their lives and some power in deciding their own destinies.[3] Every work stoppage since then seems to have somewhere within its motivation a yearning for two basic human needs: power and freedom. No human being can develop fully without them.

The formation of the medieval guilds and the occasional work stoppages that accompanied them reveal a more specific dimension to workers' motivation in their confrontations with those in authority.[4] The workers seemed to appreciate more the value of their *own* skills and take pride in their ability to produce fine objects. Consequently, they wanted a greater voice in determining their working conditions and the compensation for their work.[5] These two practical considerations seem to be part of the rationale for almost all work stoppages in the history of labor-management relations.

The Industrial Revolution

The history of modern strikes begins with Industrial Revolution in the West.[6] Because of the limitations I set for this study in the Preface, I focus primarily on the development of industrialization and striking in the United States.

About 1780 the first associations of workers were formed in the United States along craft lines in the larger population centers. "By 1790 the shoemakers and printers had organizations which can be considered the forerunners of our modern labor unions."[7] Although short-lived, Robert Owen's Grand National Consolidated Trades Union of the 1830s is indicative of the rapid progress made in organizing skilled and even some unskilled workers. Within a few weeks of its establishment, this union had enlisted more than half a million workers:

> Workers of every sort flocked into the new organization. It enrolled not only skilled craftsmen and factory operatives in the major trades, but workers in every conceivable occupation. Agricultural labourers were enrolled in many districts....Lodges of "Industrious Females" were formed in many centres, and "Miscellaneous Lodges" enlisted not only manual workers in the scattered trades, but also many sympathizers from the professional classes. The aim of the Union, in Owen's mind, was nothing less than the inclusion in one great body of the whole of the "productive classes."[8]

Common laborers were included in Owen's movement because mass production was being gradually introduced into the American scene at this time (the first rolling mill was opened in Pittsburgh, PA, in 1811; the first textile mills began operation in Lowell, MA, in 1822).[9] The comprehensive organization of unskilled laborers, however, was not a major thrust of the union movement until the Congress of Industrial Organizations (CIO) was established in 1939.[10]

The more significant and enduring (in impact, if not always in historic continuity) organizations were formed in the last half of the nineteenth century: the Knights of Labor in 1869, the Federation of Organized Trades in Pittsburgh in 1881, and the American Federation of Labor (AFL) in 1886. All of these unions were for skilled workers rather than common laborers.[11]

With the spread of workers' organizations in the new industrial society, industrial strikes became more frequent. The earliest strike recorded in U.S. history occurred in 1741 in New York ("a strike among certain bakers").[12] Local strikes by craftspersons began to occur more frequently in the early 1800s. Toward the end of the century, mass strikes against the owners of the large factories and sometimes against entire national industries began to take place.

The first reaction of capitalists, management personnel, the government, and even the general public to these early strikes is instructive to anyone interested in understanding the development of labor-management relations. All these groups considered strikes to be conspiracies:

> The very process of organization was interpreted as a *conspiracy in restraint of trade* and implied a denial of the right of the worker to increase his (or her) own wealth in his (or her) own way if that way necessitated *group action*. Between 1806 and 1842, the common law doctrine of conspiracy was invoked against workers who combined in trade-unions.[13]

An Anglican clergyman and member of a prosperous British family carried this conspiracy interpretation of strikes to an incredible extreme. To the Durham miners on strike in 1844, the Reverend John Burdon wrote: "You are resisting not the oppression of your employers but the Will of your Maker—the ordinance of that God Who has said that in the sweat of his face shall man eat bread, and Who has attached this penalty to the refusal to labour, namely, that if a man does not work neither shall he eat."[14]

Fortunately, the case of *Commonwealth v. Hunt* (1842) marked the end of the conspiracy argument as an obstacle to labor-union organization, at least as far as the legal system was concerned.[15] From a philosophical point of view, occasional articles and public statements show that some people in our society still hold this view.

Two presuppositions undergird the conspiracy argument that are subtly used against the organization of human service workers today. The first is that of "rugged individualism," i.e., that each worker should be able to confront the large corporation or even the government alone without forming worker association. Those who affirm this presupposition obviously intend to withhold any sharing of power from the workers or at least make it extremely difficult for them to gain power. The "right-to-work" laws in certain states seem to be based on a similar theory.

The second presupposition is that "free trade," which is based on the right to use one's own private property as one sees fit, should be safeguarded at any cost, even at the cost of the common worker's constitutional right to enter into free associations. In other words, this theory presumes that power belongs in the hands of those who have acquired property and position, that it is justly theirs, and that it is immoral for less successful people to organize in order to counterbalance that power. According to this second presupposition, the conspiracy theory can be seen as a practical expression of Social Darwinism.[16]

Ascent of unions to power (1850s to 1940s)

From the middle of the nineteenth century, the laws of the United States (and of England and France)[17] created an atmosphere that allowed workers to organize more freely—but never without equally free and forceful resistance—and to establish themselves as major forces in the U.S. industrial system. The resistance to this gradual establishment of power of the unions is evidenced most clearly by the regular eruptions of violence that accompanied strikes. I am not suggesting that the foes of the union movement primarily initiated the violence. I am simply pointing out that the tensions caused by this legally enforced sharing of power are manifested by the frequent incidence of violence:

> ...[B]eginning with the railroad strikes of 1877, almost every major strike for the following 40 years was attended by an outbreak of violence. By threatening the integrated philosophical value system of the business community, unionism provoked anxiety regarding the correctness of a style of life, in all its dimensions.[18]

The greatest anxiety that this new style of industrial life provoked was, Who should have the ultimate power to direct the economy of the nation?

Federal legislation shows a clear progression of thought in favor of workers' right to share in the power that shapes U.S. economic system. The Sherman Antitrust Act of 1890 sought to keep in check the tendency of powerful capitalists to take over certain markets completely. (Interestingly some employers initiated cases *against unions* for "restraint of trade" under the provisions of this act.[19]) The Railway Labor Act of 1926 required railroad employers to bargain collectively with the freely selected representatives of their workers.[20] The Norris-LaGuardia Act of 1932 prohibited the use of injunctions in labor disputes in the profit-making industries. This law was not applied to public employment where injunctions were, and still are, permitted.[21]

Perhaps the most important piece of legislation in this period that safeguarded the rights of organized labor in the U.S. economic system was the Wagner Act of 1935. This act declared that certain actions by employers would now be considered "unfair labor practices" and reason for prosecution in the U.S. courts. It established an election system through which employees could select labor unions of their choice and established the National

Labor Relations Board (NLRB), which was empowered to administer the regulations against unfair labor practices and to oversee elections for unionization.[22] Only in 1974 were private, not-for-profit organizations and institutions made subject to the provisions of this law, through Public Law 93-360. (The effects of this recent interpretation of the Wagner Act are discussed in detail in Chapter Three.)

Even though U.S. law was affirming the rights of industrial workers to share in the power of the marketplace and the major industrial unions were successful in organizing many skilled and unskilled workers,[23] strong opposition to the unions and to their ultimate weapon of striking remained in U.S. society.

I will point out two specific facets of that opposition to demonstrate, in the following chapters, some parallels that exist in the opposition to the unionization of human service workers today. Since both these "dangers" have generally been proved unfounded in the case of industrial unionization, perhaps people today be able to view the "parallel dangers" in the human service areas with less fear and more objectivity.

In the early 1900s, a pioneer student of the labor movement named Robert F. Hoxie argued "that trade-unionism and scientific management were incompatible."[24] The two forces had opposing goals and opposing methods; one would have to give in and lose its own identity. There was simply no way that two such opposing forces could cooperate in the same economic system. Many theorists today conclude that just the opposite has come to pass: the "union is now accepted as a permanent, and perhaps even a welcome, part of the enterprise."[25] Unions often accept and enforce values proposed by employers: "...many employer concepts of shop administration have been accepted in union circles. This is particularly true as to various obligations of the employee—to render continuous service...to meet established production standards, to obey instructions from supervisors, and to obey shop rules."[26] Thus, in some instances, unions relieve management of the burdensome task of enforcing management's own values.

Another form of this argument concluded that organized labor was incompatible with sound management in a capitalist system because it opposed the two principles on which the U.S. economic system had been founded: "freedom of contract" and "private property." "No amount of verbal artifice can conceal the fundamental opposition of organized labor to these two principles."[27] This reasoning argues for a radical incompatibility between unions and management, based on an absolutist interpretation of these two principles.

Through the years and after many confrontations between management and unions, experts in the field generally agree that our U.S. system is *not* based on absolutist notions of freedom of contract and the use of private property. Economists and political scientists seem to agree that these two principles must be modified, especially by a concern for the common good and for the rights of other individuals in the community.[28]

Similarly some argue today that the concerns of unions are incompatible with the idealistic goals of not-for-profit, private institutions and agencies. They believe unions set up an adversary relationship that destroys the altruism and idealism of the not-for-profit systems. Such assertions are examined in detail in the following chapters. For now, I wish to point out how similar fears existed concerning industrial unionization and how experience and careful analysis of the facts have shown them to be unfounded.

Trade unionism also was suspect through the first half of the twentieth century because of its perceived association with socialist and revolutionary movements. It is true that most "revolutionary groups have agreed that trade unions are schools and organizing centers of revolution and that strikes are a means of preparing for the violent overthrow of capitalism."[29] Even if most U.S. unions had nothing to do with revolutionary groups, it was easy to frighten an uninformed public by suggesting that unions were playing into the hands of radicals who sought to overthrow the U.S. government.

This fear was made more real by the presence of at least one revolutionary union in the United States in the first three decades of this century, the Industrial Workers of the World (IWW). This small, strident organization was founded on the principles of "syndicalism," a socialist labor movement that was strong in England and France, which sought the overthrow of capitalist systems and governments by means of national strikes.[30]

The IWW did espouse the syndicalist principle that every small strike is useful for "sharpening the inherent revolutionary potential of the workers."[31] Every strike is therefore part of a grand swelling movement that will eventually lead to the demise of capitalism and the downfall of the democratic system.

Fears that the whole union movement was revolutionary in a syndicalist sense proved irrational. Unions were victims of "guilt by perceived association" and not by real association. Rather than being revolutionaries, unions and their leaders were gradually becoming part of the capitalist system. As early as 1886, Samuel Gompers, a "totem of the U.S. labor movement," was sharply attacked by socialists for his emphasis on "trade agreements and craft organization [which] signalized an acceptance of capitalist society."[32]

Similar fears of "guilt by association" plague the union movement today as it attempts to organize and represent human service workers. Some argue that the unionization of these workers is nothing less than revolutionary and will bring about the downfall of the entire network of voluntary and charitable institutions. Unions with some instances of corruption in their past are immediately judged to be unworthy of representing people who idealistically serve others. More specifically, teachers' unions that have opposed tax credits for parochial schools are summarily judged to be unfit to represent parochial school teachers.

I am not suggesting that such considerations should not be taken into account when human service workers are considering unionization. *Any fact* should be evaluated when such an important decision is being made. I am proposing that we learn a lesson from the past and not allow irrational fears to be decisive in the question of the unionization of human service workers. No human movement has ever been flawless. Occasional corruption in the union movement should not be used to negate the concept of unionization for human service workers.

Contemporary industrial strikes: a transformed phenomenon

By 1940 the period of strike violence was over. Perhaps the call to national unity in World War II was largely responsible for this termination of violence.[33] Perhaps, too, after 150 years of experience in union organizing and striking, all parties involved were coming to a certain maturity in handling conflict in labor-management relations.

Certainly the New Deal was responsible to some significant degree for the change. More effectively than ever before, the federal government backed labor's right to organize, to bargain collectively and even to strike in an orderly fashion. The latitude and discretion that the Roosevelt administration gave to the NLRB literally forced "that sharing of power which labor had demanded."[34]

Whatever the causes, labor relations and strikes emerged as somewhat transformed phenomena in the four decades after World War II. The concerned parties (management, government, labor, the public) generally seemed to accept the balance of power that unionization and the possibility of strikes had brought to the U.S. economic and political systems.

Arthur Ross summarizes how these phenomena had settled by 1960: "[It] is well established that employers in the older industrialized countries have generally accommodated themselves to unionism and collective bargaining. Once regarded as subversive and insurrectionary, the union is now accepted as a permanent, and perhaps even a welcome, part of the enterprise."[35]

In the late 1800s and in the first half of this century, many viewed the organization of workers as a serious threat to the orderly progress of business and to the discipline of individual factories and mills. In the 1960s, union structure often began to be seen as support for a disciplined work-style, and as a means of providing orderly work services according to clearly defined contractual agreements:

> [W]here industrial relations have matured, discipline has reintegrated into collective bargaining. Principles of due process and consistency have been introduced, and on the other hand many employer concepts of shop administration have been accepted in union circles. This is particularly true as to various obligations of the employee—to render continuous service during the period of an agreement, to meet established production standards, to obey instructions from supervisors, and to observe shop rules.[36]

In this transformed milieu, labor organizations grew to the size and strength that seemed to have been the dream of such persons as Robert Owen with his Grand National Consolidated Trades Union of the 1830s. The merger of the AFL and the CIO in 1955, with George Meaney as president, was the clearest sign of the successful consolidation and strengthening of the labor movement.

The major internal conflicts that the AFL-CIO experienced within a little over a decade, the expulsion of the Teamsters in 1957 and the withdrawal of the United Auto Workers in 1968, are not necessarily signs of weakness or an incapacity to function properly. Perhaps these conflicts are more accurately understood as signs of maturing.

Although since World War II the federal government has consistently and effectively backed the organizing efforts of industrial unions and their right to demand collective bargaining, it has also sought to moderate the new power of labor organizations. The Taft-Hartley Act of 1947 declared certain union practices to be "unfair labor practices," counterbalancing what the Wagner Act (1935) had said about certain actions of management. In 1959 the Labor Management Reporting and Disclosure Act set up a code of conduct for unions and their officers to ward off possible internal corruption. This law mandated that unions make annual financial reports to the secretary of labor and disclose these reports to their members.[37] As an accepted member of the U.S. economic and political systems, unions would now be inspected and supervised, as well as supported, by the federal government.

Some economists and political philosophers make another observation to demonstrate why unions have become acceptable in modern U.S. society. The collective bargaining system supports the principles of capitalism.[38] In their struggle for greater rewards in the industrial system, unions affirm that people must be enterprising, energetic, hardworking, and clever to benefit from the system. The Socialist party was accurate in its criticism of Sam Gompers and his AFL in 1886. The union movement was not revolutionary; it simply rearranged power without disturbing the basic principles and functioning of the existing democratic capitalist system.

Many political scientists and economists had even come to view striking as a "necessary cog" in the system. The possibility of a strike provided a necessary balance to the growing power of wealthy capitalists. When practiced without violence, it became a helpful tool in pressuring agreement between otherwise recalcitrant parties. The strike is well described as follows:

[T]he mechanism which produces that increment of pressure necessary to force agreement where differences are persistent and do not yield to persuasion or argument around the bargaining table.... Thus, the strike, or threat of strike, is the ultimate device whereby the competing interests of antagonistic parties are expediently resolved, leading to a *modus operandi* which permits both sides to accommodate their differences and live with one another.[39]

The strike preserves another characteristic of the economic and political system that most U.S. citizens have been taught to treasure. It preserves as much freedom, independence, and initiative as possible on both sides of the bargaining table. "The alternative to such a system might result in the demise of the collective bargaining system as we know it; some form of coercion exercised by a supreme authority whether it be a government board, an industrial relations court, compulsory arbitrations...would supplant the voluntarism implicit in the American collective bargaining experience."[40]

The strike became such an accepted part of the system by the 1960s that it began to be ignored. Statistics compiled by Ross and Hartman indicate that a gradual and significant decrease in the phenomenon of striking occurred in the United States from 1900 to 1956.[41] This led them to include a chapter entitled "The Withering Away of the Strike" in their 1960 book.[42]

Federal employees after World War II

Public service employees working for the government were considered to be in a different category from industrial workers through the entire period of union development. The Pendleton Act of 1883 established the federal civil service system "with its guiding principle of merit, which remains the cornerstone of the system a century later."[43] Because of this system, government workers apparently felt a certain security in their positions that workers in private industry did not.[44]

Federal legislation continually reinforced this perception of a "different category" for public service workers. The Taft-Hartley Act of 1947 made into statutory law what had been a traditional presupposition of common law, i.e., that strikes by federal employees were unlawful.[45] In 1955 this provision was reinforced by stronger legislation that required federal employees to sign affidavits that they would not strike and would not join organizations that asserted a right to strike.[46]

The fact that Congress decided to pass such laws indicates that federal workers' attitudes must have been changing. Workers *were* becoming more impressed with the feasibility of striking and more convinced that they had a right to strike.

Why was the mentality of federal employees changing? Harvey Friedman, a former union official and now a professor of government, suggests that in the 1960s government workers discovered that industrial workers, skilled and unskilled, had passed them up in several important categories. Industrial workers were often making higher wages, had better benefits, had a greater voice about their working conditions, and had comparable job security. In short, they were finding that unionization, collective bargaining, and striking were more effective means for the advancement of workers than the civil service system.[47]

Senator Fred Harris of Oklahoma offered another insight. He observed that public service workers were experiencing a frustration similar to what many minority groups were articulating in the 1960s, "the frustration of powerlessness."[48] They wanted to be treated as adults, not as dependents. They wanted to be active participants in working out the terms and conditions of their service.

President Kennedy responded to this new consciousness in government workers by issuing an executive order in 1962 that granted federal employees the right to engage in collective bargaining about various conditions, primarily administrative issues, in their contracts.[49] They were not permitted, however, to raise the key issue of compensation or to strike.

Although Kennedy's executive order seemed to signal an "opening" in the federal government's approach to its employees, President Nixon's handling of the national postal strike in 1970 seemed to close whatever opening had been created. When he activated the National Guard to restore postal service in New York City and threatened to do the same in other major cities, he made history. He was the first president to use troops to quell a federal workers' strike.[50] President Reagan took even stronger action against the new consciousness of federal workers with his uncompromising stand against and consequent breaking of the Air Traffic Controllers' Union in 1981.

A decision from the U.S. District Court for the District of Columbia in 1971, affirmed by the U.S. Supreme Court in that same year, articulated the no-strike doctrine even more clearly. The Court noted that there is not and never has been "a constitutional right to strike."[51] The federal government does not act arbitrarily or irrationally, the Court declared, when it makes a no-strike promise a condition for employment. The Court stated that just reasons exist for making such a condition, including "the prerogatives of the sovereign, some sense of higher obligation associated with public service, to assure the continuing function of the Government without interruption, to protect public health and safety or for other reasons."[52]

Both in law and in their history, federal public service workers have remained in a different category from industrial workers in labor-management relations. Whether such a categorization is ethically justified is covered in the following chapters.

New phenomenon: work stoppages in human services

If the assertion is accurate that strikes were "withering away" in 1960, perhaps it was only to make the ground fallow for a unique rebirth of this pressure tactic in the next two decades. The 1960s marked the rapid development of a new phenomenon in U. S. society: work stoppages by human service workers. Organizations of teachers and nurses led the way, with police, physicians, firefighters, nursing home personnel, and other groups following closely behind.

Although some service strikes occurred before 1960, most had been in the area of "industrial services," i.e., railway workers, government printers, skilled workers in the navy yards and in army arsenals, and postal clerks.[53] Very rarely had strikes been called by persons engaged in "human services," e.g., teachers' strikes in Norwalk, CT, in 1946 and in Manchester, NH, in 1957, and the famous Boston police strike in 1919.

To clarify this discussion, I should distinguish "human" services from "industrial" services—a distinction not always made in the literature on striking. The term "human service" designates any service in which a relationship (or relationships) is essential for its delivery. Amicable relationships make any task easier; however, certain services involve human relationships as an integral part of the delivery process. I include here the services performed by such workers as teachers, nurses, physicians, counselers, clergy, and health care personnel in nursing homes. (A complete listing and categorization of service workers will be included at the end of Chapter Three.) Perhaps another adjective that would describe these services is "personal"; affective human experience is included in their very nature.

In public services like transportation, mail delivery, public utilities, support services at institutions (maintenance and food service personnel, etc.), the development of personal relationships is not essential to the task. The services are essential for smooth human functioning and for the delivery systems and industries that support human growth. Thus they are appropriately called "industrial services."

This distinction is valuable for understanding U. S. society's experience with striking until the 1960s. Before then, almost all workers in human services hesitated to strike. Those people who delivered industrial services were somewhat less hesitant. A reluctance to strike was least noticeable among workers employed by profit-making industries, especially giant industries where almost nothing personal was associated with the work.

This distinction says nothing about the rightness or wrongness of any of these groups striking. It only points out that people in society were having different reactions to the phenomenon of striking, based on the personal nature of their work. Chapter Three analyzes and interprets these experiences and attempts to draw some conclusions from them.

How and why did the new phenomenon of human service strikes begin? This question can be answered by tracing briefly the development of the unionization of the two largest groups of human service workers, teachers and nurses.[54] Rather than writing a complete history of either movement, I emphasize those facets of development that reveal the major ethical issues that belong to this new phenomenon.

Most major ethical issues can be seen in the conflicts experienced by teachers and nurses. These are reexperienced by social workers, nursing home personnel, etc. Some ethical issues, however, have surfaced only in other union conflicts, e.g., police strikes. I include those issues as they fit historically in my general review of teachers' and nurses' strikes.

In the 1950s, a strong movement developed among public employees to seek the right to bargain collectively with their employers. This movement began to have some effect in the early 1960s. For teachers, "the real beginning of the collective bargaining movement usually is associated with the New York City United Federation of Teachers winning bargaining rights in 1961."[55] This beginning received immediate and dramatic moral support from President Kennedy's executive order the following year, granting all federal employees the right to engage in collective bargaining.

Until then, although never clearly argued for or proved, a presumed principle in common law stated that human service employees should not strike.[56] Even President Roosevelt, a friend of labor through his New Deal policies, observed in 1937 that public service strikes "were unthinkable and intolerable."[57]

In the new atmosphere of the 1960s, teachers' strikes were inevitable. Not even the labor-management experts, however, expected them to come in such mushrooming numbers. In the decade of the 1970s, more than 100 teachers' strikes occurred each year in the United States, with a high of 158 in 1978-1979.[58]

The most significant ethical question to arise in this sea of conflict was "irreparable harm." Do work stoppages by teachers damage the educational process of some students in such a way that they never regain the benefits that might have been theirs? Further, do teachers' work stoppages put irreparable cracks in the educational system and make it a permanently flawed instrument for the delivery of this most important aspect of youthful development? School boards and educational philosophers also raised the question of the possible harm to other constituencies in society: vandalism by restless students, life upsets for working parents, loss of confidence by the local community in an unstable system, etc.[59]

The U.S. courts have given no consistent interpretation of the irreparable harm standard. Some courts have interpreted irreparable harm from the perspective of the traditional argument about the "sovereignty" of the state. Strong expressions of this argument against teachers' strikes can be found in the *Norwalk Teachers' Association v. Board of Education of the City of Norwalk* (1951) and in the *Buffalo Board of Education v. Pisa, New York State* (1976). Both these decisions argue that teachers' strikes deny to the state the right of sovereignty entrusted to it by a majority of the people. They maintain that the public, by free democratic process, has given the state the right to govern according to its best wisdom. Teachers usurp that authority by striking and thus cause "irreparable injury" to the democratic process.[60]

To the present day, the most common response of school boards to teachers' strikes has been to seek court injunctions forcing teachers back to work, based on their assertion that irreparable harm was taking place. Up to 1980, "among the strikes which lasted two or more days, nearly three-fourths were accompanied by board efforts almost always successful to obtain injunctive relief."[61] Management seeking injunctions in other service strikes (by police, at state institutions, etc.) has since become standard.

Other courts have taken a more moderate approach to the interpretation of the irreparable harm standard. In the case of the *School District for the City of Holland v. Holland Educational Association* (1968), the Supreme Court of Michigan ruled that the *facts* of any individual strike must demonstrate irreparable harm. To prove that a strike is illegal is not to have proven that it is causing irreparable damage to any constituency.[62]

The Supreme Court of Rhode Island gave a similar opinion in the *School Committee of Westerly v. Westerly Teachers Association* (1973). This decision states that many reasons exist for postponing or missing school days, e.g., weather, health, or damage to buildings. Thus missing some school days because of a strike is in itself not catastrophic.[63]

Although these arguments continue, more than half the states have passed legislation granting collective bargaining rights to teachers, and at least nine states have given teachers' organizations a limited right to strike.[64]

Police strikes, which began to occur in the 1970s for the first time since the 1919 Boston police strike, raised the question of irreparable harm in a different way. The harm involved here was the threat to the physical safety of citizens and the potential disruption of public order in local communities. Police unions took the issue of irreparable harm seriously and responded to situations where strikes seemed imminent by making careful plans for the protection of citizens and the maintenance of public order in the event of a strike.[65] Because of the obvious potential for harm to powerless citizens, the International Union of Police Associations has taken a firm position in favor of compulsory binding arbitration for all impasse situations in collective bargaining.

Another important court decision in 1980 forced a new issue into the spotlight concerning unionization and collective bargaining in higher education. The U.S. Supreme Court upheld Yeshiva

University's (NY) right to refuse to bargain with a faculty union in *National Labor Relations Board v. Yeshiva* (1980, no. 75-857). The Court accepted the idea that the type of activity in which the faculty was engaged was sufficient grounds for denying them coverage by the National Labor Relations Act.[66] The faculty's involvement in hiring and dismissing colleagues, shaping curriculum, setting academic policy, and granting tenure seemed to place them more on the side of management than of labor in the collective bargaining process. In effect, the court ruled that the faculty at Yeshiva was part of management.

The Yeshiva decision declared that college faculty members are "different" from other employees. Workers in a mass production plant generally have no managerial prerogatives, and little or nothing to say about policy. Thus a union clearly empowers them to have some voice about their role at the workplace. Does the power given to professionals like college faculty, through their positions on committees, etc., give them a share in a university's managerial function and thus render a union unnecessary? This is one of the questions about "difference" that is analyzed and interpreted in Chapter Three.

The development of nurses' strikes is similar to that of teachers' strikes. A move toward collective bargaining began immediately after World War II and received special impetus from the innovative California Nurses' Association, which had strong confrontations with the National War Labor Board in 1943. Consequently, the American Nurses' Association (ANA) adopted an economic security program in 1946, including an exhortation to all state and district nurses' associations to act as bargaining agents for their members. The ANA, however, in a self-reflective study of the nature of the nursing profession, adopted a no-strike policy in 1950.[67]

The 1950s and early 1960s proved to be frustrating to nurses' associations. Without the power that comes from the possibility of using pressure tactics, they found that their role as bargaining agents was feeble. They claimed that employers abstained from meaningful negotiations and simply adhered to whatever conditions they had set for the bargaining sessions.

In the early 1960s, some nurses' associations began to use mass resignations as a pressure tactic in San Francisco, Youngstown, New York City, Los Angeles, and in other areas in California and Illinois.[68] Nurses still considered strikes as unprofessional. Mass resignation was seen as a useful means for obtaining their goals "with honor."

The mass resignation tactic gradually led to an acceptance of striking as a last resort, especially when it was the only way to change a poorly functioning health care system. In 1966, the California Nurses' Association repealed its no-strike pledge. The ANA did the same in 1968, followed by the National Association of Practical Nurses in 1969.[69] After a few scattered strikes in the late 1960s, nurses' strikes began to increase both in numbers and in intensity after 1974. The longest and perhaps famous was the Ohio Nurses' Association strike at Ashtabula Hospital in 1980, which lasted 570 days.[70]

The new strength of nurses' unions and all other human service unions was enhanced in this period by the passage of Public Law 93-360 in 1974, which brought all not-for-profit institutions, public and private, under the jurisdiction of the NLRB.[71]

As the new assertiveness of nurses gradually spread to other health care workers (orderlies, aides, nursing home personnel, etc.), new ethical concerns arose for all involved in health service delivery. Two issues stood out as the most challenging.

The first issue concerns "irreparable harm" as it applies to one's total health. The issue involves much more than simply preventing people from dying. It raises the question, How much does the disruption of services at hospitals, nursing homes, clinics, or emergency rooms influence the *total well-being* of the clients accustomed to being served by them?

The second issue is more theoretical but is also more challenging, the question of a *right to health care.* Does any basis exist for concluding that such a right is innate within human beings? Conversely, would the denial of such a right frustrate basic human development? Opponents of the newly formed nurses' unions argue that nurses' strikes deprived the public of one of its most fundamental and critical rights.

The reasons for nurses' new assertiveness and that of other health care professionals were simple. Like other public service workers, they experienced the "frustration of powerlessness" already discussed. They were also painfully aware of how union workers in most other fields had passed them by, economically and professionally.

Another reason for their new assertiveness, however, stands out in many accounts of their confrontations with management. This is an extremely important consideration in the formation of a moral theology of their strikes. Nurses, more than any other human service workers, seem to have a deep sense of mission about improving the quality of the health care delivery system. As trained professionals, they are more intimately tied to the daily delivery of health care than anyone else in the system, yet they have had little or no power to shape the process.[72] They have most often been relegated to the role of "doctors' helpers" but are burdened with the continuous supervision of patients' recovery processes. Also, since nurses' salaries average less than one fourth of doctors', it is not difficult to understand why the tensions they experienced erupted in the past two decades.[73]

The nature of a strike

To give a clear, experiential description of a strike, I first should review the various stages in the development of this pressure tactic in the United States.

Initially industrial strikes were strong and often hostile actions against very powerful employers who seemed to have little concern for and understanding of their employees' needs. Because the gaps in understanding and wealth were so cavernous between management and labor and workers' frustration was so pronounced, some violence frequently accompanied these initial confrontations. The following quotation from an editorial in *The Nation* in the late 1800s concerning a violent strike in Martinsburg, WV, shows that some members of the establishment viewed strikes as battles in a long-standing war, the outcome of which would decide who would control the economic system:

> The kindest thing which can be done for the great multitudes of untaught men who have been received on these shores, and are daily arriving, and who are torn perhaps even more here than in Europe by wild desires and wilder dreams, is to show them promptly that society as here organized, on individual freedom of thought and action, is impregnable, and can be no more shaken than the order of nature. The most cruel thing is to let them suppose, even for one week, that if they had only chosen their time better, or had been better led or better armed, they would have succeeded in forcing it to capitulate...it would be fatal to private and public

> credit and security to allow a state of things to subsist in
> which 8,000 or 9,000 day-laborers of the lowest class can
> suspend, even for a whole day, the traffic and industry of
> a great nation, merely as a means of extorting ten or twenty
> cents a day more wages from their employers...[74]

The most radical interpreters of strikes, around the turn of the twentieth century, saw them as steps toward a socialist revolution that would eventually bring the democratic capitalist system to its knees. This view received little support from U.S. trade unionists and gradually faded by the 1920s.

In the first half of this century, most involved parties viewed a strike as an economic pressure tactic used by workers in order to force industrial owners and managers to concede to their demands. By World War II the violence of previous striking was subsiding but the atmosphere surrounding strikes was still hostile. After World War II the tone of strikes transformed significantly. A strike, and especially the threat of one, came to be accepted as a necessary "cog in the wheel," a mechanism to help keep everyone honest at the bargaining table.

Perhaps a contrast of metaphors would help to convey this transformed notion of a strike. The strike is no longer a weapon of battle between two factions at war that will leave a winner and a loser. The strike is now a tool for maneuvering between two competitors in the same system, each seeking a position of strength in that system where both will continue to live and work together.

The definition of a strike in *Roberts' Dictionary of Industrial Relations* describes well this final stage in the development of industrial strikes:

> A temporary stoppage of work or concerted withdrawal from
> work by a group of employees of an establishment or several
> establishments to express a grievance or to enforce demands
> affecting wages, hours and/or working conditions. It is a con-
> certed withdrawal of work since it is the action of a group,
> and it is a temporary withdrawal since the employees expect
> to return to work after the dispute has been resolved.[75]

To make the definition more experiential, we could describe the mindset of the workers as they go through the process of striking in the following way:

1. We need to put pressure on management. They are not responding to our needs.

2. We will stop working. We will shut down the smoothly functioning system that they have set up and they control.

3. With the system shut down, they will gain no profit from their investment. They will gain no benefits from the system until we decide to return to work.

4. We presume that no one else will supply the work that we are not doing. We will exert pressure to ensure that no one does the work that we have stopped.

5. We presume that, when the dispute is settled, we will return to the same jobs that we had before. We will resume our work according to the conditions of our new agreement.

Such a confrontation brings a balance of power to industry. Owners cannot make a profit unless their employees work. Employees cannot live a decent life unless the owners agree to pay them a just portion of the rewards of the industrial enterprise.

An admirable directness exists in the confrontation here. The owners and managers who control the system are directly pressured by the job action of the workers. They must face the pressure and respond. The employees forego their salary for the duration of the strike, willing to give up this short-term benefit for long-term goals.

In human service strikes, the clear lines of confrontation are blurred by the presence of a third party, the client. How accurately does the previous description of an industrial strike fit a concerted withdrawal of work in human services? Are there new dimensions to the experience of striking in human services that affect the ethical evaluation of the phenomenon? These are some of the questions addressed in the next chapter.

Notes

1. K.G. Knowles, *Strikes* (Oxford: Basil Blackwell, 1952), p. 2.

2. Donald A. McLean, *The Morality of the Strike* (New York: P.J. Kenedy & Sons, 1921), pp. 9-10.

3. Knowles, p. 2.

4. McLean, pp. 9-10, 12; see also Thomas S. Adams and Helen Sumner, *Labor Problems* (New York: Macmillan, 1905), p. 177.

5. McLean, p. 10.

6. The Industrial Revolution begins at the turn of eighteenth century in England. Shortly thereafter, it spreads to the United States. John

A. Garraty and Peter Gay, eds., *The Columbia History of the World* (New York: Harper & Row, Publishers, Inc., 1972), pp. 822-847.

7. Robert E. Walsh, "Background of an Issue," in R.E. Walsh, ed., *Sorry...No Government Today* (Boston: Beacon Press, 1969), p. 5.

8. Arthur M. Ross, "The Natural History of the Strike," in A. Kornhauser, R. Dubin, and A. Ross, eds., *Industrial Conflict* (New York: McGraw-Hill, 1954), p. 25.

9. Garraty and Gay, p. 823.

10. Garraty and Gay, p. 11.

11. Garraty and Gay, p. 6.

12. Adams and Sumner, p. 177.

13. Theresa Wolfson, "Social Control of Industrial Conflict," in A. Kornhauser, R. Dubin, and A. Ross, eds., *Industrial Conflict* (New York: McGraw-Hill, 1954), p. 4.

14. Knowles, p. 4.

15. Wolfson, p. 410.

16. Social Darwinism is a theory of social progress fashioned by conservative spokespersons for private capitalism in the second half of the nineteenth century in the United States. This theory holds that there is a process of "natural selection" in social and economic affairs as well as in biological evolution. Those who become rich and successful do so because they have used their superior native talents well. It is natural, fitting, and just that they should have greater rewards than those who are less talented and apparently less fit. See Garraty and Gay, pp. 958-960.

17. Knowles, p. 5; McLean, p. 14.

18. Daniel Bell, "Industrial Conflict and Public Opinion," in A. Kornhauser, R. Dubin, and A. Ross, eds., *Industrial Conflict* (New York: McGraw-Hill, 1954), p. 243.

19. Wolfson, p. 410.

20. Wolfson, p. 411.

21. Labor Law Course, 24th ed., CCH Editorial Staff Publication (Chicago: Commercial Clearing House, Inc., 1979), p. 5910.

22. Walsh, pp. 9-10; Bell, p. 244.

23. The newly formed Congress of Industrial Organizations (CIO) in 1939 struggled to organize workers by industry rather than by craft so that the unskilled workers would not be left out. Walsh, p. 10.

24. A. Kornhauser, R. Dubin, and A. Ross, "Alternative Roads Ahead," in *Industrial Conflict* (New York: McGraw-Hill, 1954), p. 509.

25. Arthur M. Ross and Paul T. Hartman, *Changing Patterns of Industrial Conflict* (New York: John Wiley & Sons, Inc., 1960), p. 47.

26. Ross and Hartman, p. 49.

27. Samuel Yellen, *American Labor Struggles* (New York: S.A. Russell, 1936), p. xiii.

28. David E. Apter, "Government," in *International Encyclopedia of the Social Sciences* (New York: Macmillan Co., 1968), pp. 216-219.

29. Ross, p. 27; see also Philip Taft, "Ideologies and Industrial Conflict," in A. Kornhauser, R. Dubin, and A. Ross, eds., *Industrial Conflict* (New York: McGraw-Hill, 1954), pp. 257-265.

30. Bell, p. 242; Knowles, p. 4; Taft, pp. 259-260.

31. Ross and Hartman, p. 57.

32. Bell, p. 243.

33. Bell, p. 246.

34. Bell, p. 244.

35. Ross and Hartman, p. 47.

36. Ross and Hartman, p. 49.

37. Walsh, p. 11.

38. Frederick H. Harbison, "Collective Bargaining and American Capitalism," in A. Kornhauser, R. Dubin, and A. Ross, eds., *Industrial Conflict* (New York: McGraw-Hill, 1954), p. 278.

39. Bernard Karsh, *Diary of a Strike* (Urbana, IL: University of Illinois Press, 1958), p. 13.

40. Karsh, p. 13. *(Author's note*: I take exception to authors' writing "American" when they mean United States. Karsh is referring here only to the U.S. experience and should so indicate. Throughout the book, I use the adjective "U.S." both to be precise and to be careful not to offend our northern and southern neighbors by presuming that they are *not* part of a genuinely "American" experience.)

41. Ross and Hartman, pp. 15-33.

42. Ross and Hartman, pp. 42-61.

43. Sar A. Levitan and Alexandra B. Noden, *Working for the Sovereign: Employee Relations in the Federal Government* (Baltimore, MD: Johns Hopkins University Press, 1983), p. 3.

44. Harvey L. Friedman, "The Role of the AFL-CIO in the Growth of Public Sector Collective Bargaining," in R.E. Walsh, ed., *Sorry...No Government Today* (Boston: Beacon Press, 1969), p. 29.

45. Murray B. Nesbitt, Labor Relations in the Federal Government Service (Washington, DC: Bureau of National Affairs, Inc., 1976), p. 367. In the preceding year (1954), in legislation introduced by Senator Joseph Ball of Minnesota (Public Law 419), such a position had already been taken in the form of "riders" to the bill. These riders forbade the use of any funds appropriated by the bill for paying the salary of

an employee who belonged to an organization "asserting the right to strike against the United States." In addition, employees were required to file affidavits with their department heads declaring that they were not members of such organizations, that they would not join such organizations, and that they would not strike against the United States. The Taft-Hartley Act contained no provision requiring public employees to file no-strike affidavits, but Public Law 330 in 1955 reinstated the mandate for such affidavits.

46. Nesbitt, p. 363.

47. Friedman, p. 29.

48. Richard P. McLaughlin, "Public Employee Collective Bargaining," in R.E. Walsh, ed., *Sorry...No Government Today* (Boston: Beacon Press, 1969), p. 292.

49. This was Executive Order 10988, issued on Jan. 17, 1962. See Levitan and Noden, pp. 4-6; and Nathaniel Goldfinger, "The Growth of the AFL-CIO," in R.E. Walsh, ed., *Sorry...No Government Today* (Boston: Beacon Press, 1969), pp. 16-18, for a discussion of the implications and effects of this executive order.

50. Nesbitt, p. 389.

51. *United Federation of Postal Clerks v. Blount*, 325 F. Supp. 879 (D.D.C., 1971).

52. *United Federation...v. Blount*, 325 F. Supp. 882. See Nesbitt, pp. 392-394, for a detailed summary of this decision.

53. Nesbitt, pp. 367-369.

54. By 1950, one fifth of the labor force in the United States was made up of service workers. Within this group, teachers form the largest single category of civilian employees. See David L. Colton and Edith E. Graber, *Enjoining Teacher Strikes* (St. Louis: Center for the Study of Law in Education, Washington University, 1980), p. 5.

55. Colton and Graber, p. 5.

56. Colton and Graber, p. 7.

57. Colton and Graber, p. 9.

58. Colton and Graber, p. 1.

59. The Center for the Study of Law in Education at Washington University in St. Louis did a comprehensive study of the question of "irreparable harm" that was completed in 1980. Much of the information and theory that I present in this book comes from this study.

60. David L. Colton, *Statutory Provisions for Injunctive Relief in Teacher Strikes* (St. Louis: Center for the Study of Law in Education, Washington University, 1980), pp. 10, 19.

61. Colton and Graber, p. 1.

62. Colton, p. 13.

63. See Susan Frelich Appleton, *Appellate Review of Proceedings to Enjoin Teachers' Strikes* (St. Louis, Center for the Study of Law in Education, Washington University, 1980), p. 11; see also Colton, p. 20.

64. *State Public Sector Labor Relations: A Summary, Together with Selected Notes on Recent Developments*, compiled by the Department of Organization and Field Services and the Public Employees Department of the AFL-CIO, 1984.

65. William D. Gentel and Martha L. Handman, *Police Strikes: Causes and Prevention* (Washington, DC: International Association of Chiefs of Police, Inc., 1979).

66. "Court Says College Unions Not Covered by Labor Law," *The New York Times* (Feb. 21, 1980), pp. A1, A20.

67. Norman Metzger, Joseph M. Ferentino, and Kenneth F. Kruger, *When Health Care Employees Strike* (Rockville, MD: Aspen Systems Corp., 1984), p. 94.

68. Metzger, Ferentino, and Kruger, p. 95.

69. Metzger, Ferentino, and Kruger, pp. 93-98.

70. Metzger, Ferentino, and Kruger, p. 33.

71. Metzger, Ferentino, and Kruger, pp. 3 and 18.

72. Metzger, Ferentino, and Kruger, pp. 98-99.

73. Metzger, Ferentino, and Kruger, p. 92.

74. From an editorial, "The Last Riots," in *The Nation* (Aug. 2, 1877).

75. Harold S. *Roberts' Dictionary of Industrial Relations* (Washington, DC: BNA Inc., 1966), p. 407.

Chapter 3

The Transfer from Industry to Human Services

The modern strike was developed in the forum of profit-making industry. An "industrial mold" was cast for strikes in the first 150 years of labor-management conflict in the United States. The question this chapter attempts to answer is: Can labor-management conflicts in the forum of human services be poured into that mold? Will they fit rather neatly into it, or does the mold need to be significantly redesigned?

In attempting to answer this question, I call the reader's attention again to the basic premise in Chapter One about the nature of contemporary theology. A major source for theology is *human experience.* Theology is not simply logical reasoning based on Christian Scripture. It is also an attempt to describe human experience accurately and then reflect on that experience in the light of Christian revelation.

We therefore must ask, Are the experiences of all the participants in a human service strike the same as the experiences of workers, managers, owners, and the general public when an industrial strike occurs? Simply taking the language of the industrial strike, looking for correlatives in the human service strike, and applying the language to them does not help. Such a process will obscure rather than clarify the reality.

For example, we could hardly use the word "strikebreaker" in the same sense for Pinkerton men who came down the Monongahela River to McKeesport to disrupt with physical violence the Homestead Steel strike of 1892[1] and for a 70-year-old volunteer doing chores for some friends at a nursing home during a strike by health care personnel. The intention, method, and degree of involvement of the elderly volunteer *is* a markedly different experience.

One similarity does exist in the conduct of the elderly volunteer and the Pinkerton men: both are interfering with a strike. Using "strikebreaker" for both without making major qualifications, however, can bring heated responses to cloud the issue rather than reasonable reflection to clarify it. In other words, if actions are 90 percent different and 10 percent similar, the same terms should not be used to describe them. Thus I am careful to be *descriptive* rather than *judgmental* when choosing terms in this chapter.

Union hesitation about a "difference"

In the interviews I conducted with union leaders and workers and in the "advocacy" literature in behalf of unions, an almost universal tendency exists to assert that there is "no real difference" between human service and industrial strikes. In the interviews the assertion sometimes took the form of "no essential difference" or "no substantial difference." On other occasions statements were even stronger in negating any difference: "...any harm to the clients is purely incidental" or "...service strikes are no different—it's simply a case of the workers versus their bosses, nothing else."

Union advocacy literature often argues that it is mere semantics to call human service systems professional enterprises instead of businesses. Union activist Charles Cogen writes: "Teaching, they [some educators] say, is a profession and education is not a business...semantic arguments of this sort advance us very little."[2] It seems somewhat precipitous to erase all significant distinctions between a "profession" that is established to educate people and a "business" that is established to make a profit by calling any distinction "semantics."

Cogen continues his attempt to deny any difference between schools and regular business enterprises by arguing that schools in some sense are part of the profit-making schema of things in the United States. "The 'non-profit' argument, too, is fallacious. Schools are just as much in the marketplace for their share of consumer dollars as any manufacturer of automobiles or safety pins."[3] Once again the argument for sameness seems forced. People manufacture safety pins in order to make a profit, not to perfect the "ideal safety pin" (unless it would sell better). They would cease manufacturing them if it were not profitable. School boards and educators, however, seek more funds not for personal profit but to perfect the educational system. If they go "into the red," educators will still do their best to deliver the service. Profit-on-investment is not a motivator in the educational system, but it is the prime and sometimes sole motivator in ordinary business.

An American Federation of Teachers (AFT) staff member makes the same sweeping assertion: "The employer-employee relationship has the same thrust whether the employer is an individual, a corporation, a government, a social agency, or a union....It doesn't matter who the employer happens to be."[4] Such a statement is too absolute and universal when one considers the many different kinds of employer-employee relationships. It would be difficult to imagine that working for one fair-minded individual who had set up an inner-city counseling clinic would be the same as working for a giant corporation that manufactures luxury items. An idealistic health care professional would probably have a very different employer relationship in a for-profit hospital chain that concentrates on profitable services (e.g., elective surgery) and paying customers than in a not-for-profit, voluntary hospital that emphasizes those services truly needed by patients, rich or poor.

Why are union advocates so intent to prove that no difference exists between delivering human services and working for a profit-making industry and, consequently, that no substantial difference exists between a human service strike and an industrial strike? From my research and especially from my interviews, I have come to the conclusion that three fears, conscious or unconscious, cause such a strong reaction among union advocates when the question of "difference" is raised. I raise the issue now to diffuse those fears before entering into the specifics of the moral discussion of strikes. I hope to demonstrate that nothing antiunion (or antimanagement or antistrike) is involved suggesting that human service strikes are very different from industrial strikes.

The first fear that I perceive in the reaction of union advocates is: if one can show that human service strikes are different from industrial strikes, perhaps one is implying that human service strikes are always wrong and that these workers should never strike. This is not a reasonable fear. To indicate some differences leads only to the conclusion that one must consider different values and evaluate different tensions in making ethical decisions

about human service strikes. It does not mean that one can absolutely conclude that industrial workers can strike but human
service workers cannot.

The second fear is: if human service workers are considered
different in some ways from industrial workers, they are auto-
matically being proclaimed "better," or "superior," or "above the
common laborer." Union advocates sense that an argument for
difference is an argument for elitism. This fear is indeed legitimate,
for such a process occurs frequently. As a former union official
Harvey Friedman points out, a government worker 20 years ago
typically felt "that he was part of the middle class. He did not
view himself as being a 'wage' worker.... They were more interested in developing and maintaining the prestige of their jobs"
than in joining unions.[5] Craft and industrial workers naturally
resented such an attitude. They rightfully saw it as a form of snob-
bery and as divisive to mutual understanding and assistance among
workers.

Such a snobbish attitude is not the necessary consequence
of finding some differences in the makeup of various workers'
relationship to their work. It is just as unrealistic to deny differences as it is to presume that difference equals superiority. (We
should have learned much about this issue from present confrontations over ethnicity and race.) To assert some difference between
the industrial worker's mode of operation and that of the service
worker is to describe a fact, not to make a value judgment.

Third, some union leaders may think that human service
workers, if they claim to be different, are saying to them, "Your
hard-earned expertise, gained through years of sweat and struggle, doesn't apply to us." Some union experts may fear that their
wisdom and skills are being declared worthless by this uppity
group of professionals.

To address this fear, I must first state the obvious: teachers,
nurses, physicians, etc., would be foolish to dismiss such valuable
experience, and it would be their loss. The wisdom and skills of
union leaders in the profit-making industries, especially in the
areas of organizing and bargaining, can be of great practical value
even to the most brilliant professor of philosophy.

On the other hand, union leaders would be rash to presume
that all of their wisdom and skills address the labor-management
problems of human service workers in the same way that they

have addressed industrial labor-management problems in the past. Union leaders must have some of the same humility that they ask of professional workers and admit that the answers that they have taken years to carve out in the steel industry may not fit the problems of a nurse in the intensive care unit.

The attempt to point out some differences between human service strikes and industrial strikes is not, in any sense, an argument for promoting elitism, prohibiting human service strikes, or demeaning the collective wisdom of union leaders. It is rather a struggle to discover helpful insights about a difficult and complex human experience.

Two basic differences

In the five-step description of an industrial strike presented at the cnd of Chapter Two, the first two steps are apparently the same in a human service strike: (1) workers conclude that they have no alternative other than to use a pressure tactic in dealing with management; and (2) they will stop working in order to shut down the system that management controls. In step three, however, a change occurs. Instead of applying pressure to management by ensuring that the owners and managers gain no profit from their investment, the human service strike applies pressure to management by ensuring that the service is not delivered in the system. Human service workers rightly presume that management is as interested in the delivery of the service as the workers. Otherwise a work stoppage would put little pressure on management.

In step three the interests and needs of a third party have entered into the strike experience. In human services, a client is always *immediately* involved. The public as consumers are involved indirectly in every industrial strike, but the involvement is usually so indirect and minimal as to be insignificant. For example, if Ford workers are out on strike, consumers can buy similar products from General Motors. Rather than "breaking the strike," such action by consumers heightens the strike's pressure. The owners are making no profit, the workers continue their pressure, and the public is contented and has no reason to oppose the workers' job action.

Only in a national strike would consumers be severely affected by the work stoppage. If no automobiles were being manufactured, no coal was being mined, etc., eventually everyone would feel the pressure. Even in national strikes, however, most consumers would not feel the *immediate* effect that clients would when a human service is withdrawn. Several days or weeks would pass before the full effects of a national strike would begin to touch most consumers. National strikes generally have not been a major problem in the United States, where union bargaining is carried out in a more decentralized way than in almost any other Western nation.[6]

From these examples of industrial strikes, we can note how the situation changes in human service strikes. If the clients receive the service from others (e.g., students are taught, patients are fully nursed), the effect of the strike begins to be diffused. The pressure on management is lessened somewhat because the service is being delivered.

This reflection leads us to see how step four in the description of an industrial strike is altered in a human service strike. In step four workers in industry presume that no one will supply the work for their employers; such a substitution would simply be "strike breaking." If management is to be pressured, others must not step in and keep their industries going.

Do human service workers have the same presumption in their strikes? Here the issue becomes more complex. They presume that no one should directly intervene and help management; however, they also presume that certain crucial services must be provided during a strike. Some unions try to determine which services are crucial and then supply them themselves. In many nurses' strikes and police strikes, such preparations have become an ordinary part of the process.

Do human service workers presume that clients will not seek services from other workers or from family members and friends? For example, the family could pay for a private-duty nurse, high-school students could have special college-board tutoring sessions organized for them, and friends of senior citizens could go to nursing homes to care for them. What is so different from industrial strikes in these cases is that the person supplying the service can say and sincerely *mean*, "I am intending to help the client, not support management." The two results are often so intertwined, however, that it is difficult to separate them.

Industrial strikers generally do not have to face such a dilemma. The confrontation is clear-cut in their strikes. If others supply the work of industrial strikers, these outsiders help the owners and managers to keep business functioning as usual and allow the owners to continue to make a profit on their investment. In human service strikes, new questions arise. Should clients be completely free to seek services elsewhere or invite others into the work space to supply the service? Should family and friends be free to supply services that they consider necessary and that the striking workers are not providing? These questions bring up ethical considerations that were not present in the history of industrial strikes.

The description of "differences" offered thus far depends heavily on the assertion that a fundamental and innate difference exists in intention, attitude, and method between profit and not-for-profit enterprises. Studies of the recent phenomenon of for-profit hospitals illustrate that the assertion is basically true. When public or religious hospitals are taken over by for-profit corporations like Humana, Inc., the Hospital Corporation of America, or the American Medical International, certain changes have predictably occurred. This is a fact, not a judgment on these corporations.

The data from recent studies indicate that for-profit hospitals tend to drop units or services that are not self-supporting (e.g., burn units, units for the chronically ill and elderly, rehabilitation centers).[7] Evidence suggests that the for-profit hospitals focus on serving patients who can pay in full, while discouraging, transferring, and even turning away indigent patients.[8] In the state of Florida, for example, where for-profit hospitals make up nearly 50 percent of all hospital care, such hospitals account for only 4.2 percent of the state's hospital care for the poor.[9]

This brief discussion of for-profit hospitals merely indicates that significant differences exist in the functioning of for-profit and not-for-profit systems. It seems fair to conclude, therefore, that differences also will exist between strikes in these two systems.

Position of the client

From the previous description of a human service strike, much of the difference from an industrial strike clearly involves a client (student, patient, nursing home resident, etc.) who is caught in the middle of a conflict between workers and management. Besides those already mentioned, two other observations about the client's position give rise to new considerations in determining the morality of a human service strike.

One commentator raises the question: "Who speaks for the clients?"[10] A realistic response to this question is that everyone claims to do so, but no one really does so unbiasedly. Unions generally have real concerns for their clients and wish to improve their services to them. By instituting the system, management has expressed a concrete interest in serving the clients and generally wishes to carry out this concern. Government services are legally constructed so that the board of directors represents the clients and the community, but this is hardly the fact of the matter. Board members often represent the interests that they bring from their own professions and corporations.

In the conflicts that arise in the collective bargaining process, both sides have their own interests. Besides the delivery of the service, workers must be concerned about their salaries, the benefits so necessary for their own families, their work schedules, adequate time off, their union's strength, etc. These are just concerns and should be pursued by the workers.

Besides delivery of the service, management must be concerned about the cost efficiency of the system, the retention of sufficient control to manage the system wisely, meeting the demands of the board of directors, the preservation of their own jobs, etc. These, too, are just concerns and should be pursued by management. Thus both parties have an authentic concern for the clients, and both parties have their own interests.

In an ideal world we could imagine situations in which either management or workers would be so at one with the clients that no conflict would exist between their needs and the clients' needs; one or the other would represent the clients' wishes perfectly. We do not live in an ideal world, however; for either group to represent the clients' position without bias is almost impossible.

An interesting example of this third-party interest not being served has been the occasional "student strike" after the board and the unions had resolved the teachers' strike. These students felt deprived of their freedom to celebrate holidays because of make-up days during Christmas and Easter vacations and were frustrated at the delay in their search for summer jobs. By being forced to make up school days lost by teachers' strikes, they perceived that concerns important to them were being summarily dismissed. Whether their concerns were objectively important and whether they had a right to strike and not attend school is not the point. The focus here is that no advocate was present in the collective bargaining process for third-party (client) interests.

A second observation about the client's position that leads to different considerations about human service strikes concerns the relationships between clients and workers. In most industrial enterprises, workers have little or no personal relationship with consumers, e.g., auto workers have no necessary relationship with the people who buy the cars they manufacture. Even in those cases in which the consumer and worker come to know one another, the quality of the relationship is not crucial; if an auto mechanic is skillful and efficient, most consumers will be satisfied even if the person has little capacity for relating to them.

In most human services, the situation is the opposite. For teachers, nurses, social workers, counselors, health care personnel at nursing homes, and police (some statistics show that 70 to 80 percent of an ordinary policeperson's work deals with domestic and personal relations), relationships with clients are the essence of their work. Teachers who relate well to students and nurses who have a genuine rapport with patients have a special crisis to face during strikes that is foreign to the steelworker or the carpenter: What will be the effect on the relationship with the student or patient if services are withheld? Once again, this consideration does not rule out striking. It simply adds another dimension and responsibility that all the parties involved must face when a strike by human service workers is being considered.

Position of workers and management

In the collective bargaining process and in the event of strikes, the relationship between workers and management is much the same for industrial and human service work. Management and unions are engaged in discussions about how much power each group should have and how much control each should have over the work process. Both are naturally interested in protecting and extending their own prerogatives. Both know that neither side's primary focus is to protect and develop the other's interests; it is simply not the function of either side to do so.[11] Both know that they must compromise (Frederick Harbison calls it "treaty making") if they are to continue to work together.[12]

Some new facets of worker-management relations arise in human service enterprises, however, that are not present in profit-making industries. As already seen, both workers and management must consider the client's needs as they attempt to resolve their own differences. Because of this consideration, neither side is as free to pursue its own ends as it would be in a profit-making industry. This consideration places a greater burden on the workers than on management for two reasons.

First, the human service workers naturally experience a great concern for their personal relationships with the client. They are usually in daily contact with their clients; management ordinarily is not. This concern is even stronger if the service involves a relationship that will continue for many years, e.g., in a nursing home, in an educational system, or in a physician-patient relationship.

Second, the human service workers in frequent contact with their clients will inevitably have difficulty gaining complete solidarity of position during a strike. Since the relationship with clients is personal, each human service worker will often want to make the decision personally about whether to continue the service. Some teachers and school counselors have decided on their own to tutor seniors preparing for college during a strike, much to the chagrin of other striking teachers. Some nurses have chosen to continue their work at nursing homes and hospitals during a strike. On several occasions police have made similar decisions.[13]

Industrial workers do not face this kind of tension. For them, to remain at work during a strike would be clearly supporting the owners and managers. Human service workers, on the other hand, can simultaneously be strongly opposed to the positions of management and yet feel intensely drawn to serve the people with whom they have developed authentic relationships.

Another difference can be seen in the nature of the collective bargaining process, as developed primarily for the industrial scene. Arthur Ross and Paul Hartman, referring to the writings of the pioneer social scientist of the nineteenth century, William Graham Sumner, describe the process as the union's absorbing the principles and the approach of the market system. In the market system of economics, capitalists "test the market" to discover how much they can get out of it. They push their prices to the limit that the consumer will pay. Collective bargaining and the strike, "rationally begun and rationally conducted...does the same thing for wage-earning interests."[14]

Professor Anthony Cresswell makes the same point in a more popular way: "If one gains a dollar, someone loses a dollar; it's strictly win or lose."[15] Thus, many social scientists speak of collective bargaining as a process for resolving "the problems imposed by labor's and management's divergent aims."[16]

"Divergent aims" expresses accurately what many industrial workers think about their relationship with company owners. Owners and workers stand on opposite sides of a large "pile" in the middle, the profits, and they pull in opposite directions, hoping to move larger portions of it in their own direction. "Divergent aims" does not exactly fit the experience of the human service worker in a not-for-profit enterprise in exactly the same way.

Management and workers ordinarily have entered the human service enterprise with similar aims, i.e., the delivery of a service in which they have a great interest. Often both have such strong interests in the delivery system itself that major confrontations in the collective bargaining process develop about how best to teach students, how to care for patients most effectively, etc. By contrast, industrial unions rarely have conflicts with management because they believe that they have a better way to manufacture the product. I do not say this disparagingly of industrial unions. Workers in industry certainly have an interest in developing better ways to manufacture steel, etc., but this interest is not sufficiently crucial to be the reason for a strike; they are not paid for creative involvement. On the other hand, some of the first nursing strikes (and the mass resignations that preceded them) were precisely over the issue of the quality of service. Nurses were refusing to take part in what they perceived to be mediocre health care.[17]

Certainly a major issue in the bargaining process for human service workers is compensation. They expect to earn a decent income that will support a dignified life-style. A difference also exists here, however, in how the contest for higher wages occurs. The parties are not struggling over profits. If the human service worker demands higher compensation, the demand will not lessen the owner's profit. Rather, it will force everyone to review the funding for the whole system, determine if additional funds can be made available, discover if the allocation of funds could be redistributed to meet an increase in wages. Workers are not pressuring owners for a share of their profits. They are pressuring a funding system, usually from taxes, free contributions or fees-for-service, and together with management they must face the limitations of their system.

Some social scientists point out that a strike threat gives public service workers a dimension of power that it does not give industrial workers. In industry, the pressure tactics of management that correspond to strikes by workers are lockouts, relocations, or simply closing the plant and doing something else with one's capital investment. These alternatives are generally not options for public employers and are not viable options for voluntary charitable employers.[18] Local government cannot simply drop police service or garbage collection without making some other provisions. A city hospital, especially if it is the only one in town, cannot simply close without some plan for alternative service. "Therefore it is quite possible that the loss to public employees of their . . . ultimate threat—the right to strike—may be offset by the unavailability to public employers of bargaining weapons commonly used by their colleagues in the private sector."[19]

Perhaps this lack of an ultimate weapon for management was responsible for, consciously or unconsciously, the common law tradition of no strikes by public employees. Perhaps this same fact is influential in leading the concerned parties today to what seems to be a more reasonable solution to impasses in public sector bargaining than the no-strike mandate, i.e., some form of compulsory binding arbitration. In such an arrangement, both parties face the same pressure to arrive at a settlement and are faced with the same alternatives if they cannot come to one by themselves.

The Supreme Court's decision in the Yeshiva University case, referred to in Chapter Two, points to another difference between human service workers (especially those in higher education) and industrial workers.[20] The court decided that, through committees and other consultative roles, the faculty already had such a voice in administrative decisions (hiring, granting of tenure, setting academic courses, etc.) that they could not be regarded as employees in the ordinary sense. The faculty at Yeshiva therefore was not covered by the stipulations of the National Labor Relations Act.

Any human service professionals who work in a system in which they serve on decision-making committees or advisory committees that exercise real influence already have a different relationship with their employers than laborers who are simply given the conditions of their employment. College educators, physicians, and some other health care personnel are frequently in such a position.

Pointing out this difference does not mean that I necessarily agree with the Yeshiva decision from an ethical point of view or think that such professionals should never organize into unions. Rather, it illustrates an approach to unionization, collective bargaining, and striking suggested in the recent self-study by the AFL-CIO's Committee on the Evolution of Work. The study states that "unions should experiment with new approaches to represent workers," especially those who "wish to forward their interests in ways other than what they view as the traditional form of union representation—in their view, an adversarial collective bargaining relationship."[21] Perhaps the combined experience of traditional union personnel and human service professionals in their committee and consultation roles can lead to creative new ways of dealing with the tensions that inevitably arise in worker-management relations.

One final difference exists between the areas of industry and human services that I can only suggest rather than demonstrate. I believe my suggestion will resonate with the experiences of many persons in profit-making industries and the not-for-profit human service enterprises. It deals with the difference between competition and collaboration.

The U.S. free enterprise system places great value on competition.[22] The system rewards most generously those who function best in situations with both winners and losers. Trade unions, collective bargaining, and strikes have grown up within that capitalist system. By osmosis, unions and their strategies have come to share in the capitalist spirit that values competitive skills and presumes that competitiveness is one of the final goals of human development. Is this person a good competitor? If so, then that person has matured and has developed into a valuable human being.

Not all professionals share the notion that competitive development is healthful human growth. Belgian psychologist H.

Nouwen sees the spirit of competition as being positively destructive in certain areas of human pursuit. "Competition has become one of the most pervasive and also destructive aspects of modern education....It is obvious that in a system that encourages this ongoing competition, knowledge no longer is a gift that should be shared, but a property that should be defended."[23]

Collaboration, not competition, more frequently sets the tone for work in human services, although some competitive structures are present. The valuing of competition is not as pronounced, or as overt, however, as it is in capitalist industry. Concerns for serving, sharing, and collaborating are special values among most human service personnel, even though they do not always act on these values.

Some of the resistance to unionization, collective bargaining, and striking in human services may come from an antipathy to the strong sense of competition that the labor movement has absorbed from the free enterprise system. A new awareness of the tension between the competitive spirit of capitalism and the collaborative spirit of human service enterprises may be emerging in the U.S. labor movement. Statements like the following from the AFL-CIO self-study seem to reflect such an awareness:

> [A] bargaining approach based on solving problems through arbitration or mediation rather than through ultimate recourse to economic weapons may be most effective....[24]
> ...a new orthodoxy is the precise opposite of the proper approach. Collective bargaining is not, and should not be, confined by any rigid and narrow formula....It is the special responsibility of the individual unions to make creative use of the collective bargaining concept and to adapt bargaining to these times and to the present circumstances.[25]

Some managers of charitable and religious institutions have objected to unionization of their workers because they thought that unions had "different values" than the institutions and that community would be more difficult to form if their workers became unionized. This objection has seemed absurd to those familiar with the labor movement's concern each worker's dignity and for justice and fairness for those who were powerless. How could these values be different from those espoused by most religious and humanitarian institutions? The objection was probably expressing the instinctive sense that unions reflect too thoroughly capitalist values, especially the competitive spirit that many argue fits poorly in the area of human services.

This emphasis on competition reflects once again how unionization, collective bargaining, and striking have been developed almost completely from a male perspective. In her studies of how men and women have been socialized to view life differently, Carol Gilligan points out how competition is not highly valued by women.[26] Gilligan refers to a study by Janet Lever of the play patterns of fifth-grade girls and boys. Boys were extremely interested in setting exact rules and fighting to ensure that everyone followed them perfectly. If some boys could not achieve success because of the rigidity of the rules, that was all right. Everyone knew the rules when the game started, had the same chance to succeed, and had to follow them in the same way.

The girls were much more tolerant in their attitudes toward the rules of the game and competition. If the rules caused too much argument, the girls reinterpreted them. If some players could not succeed because of the rules' rigidity, they changed them. If the competition caused serious arguments, they stopped the game. The players were obviously more important than the rules; their relationships were more important than successful competition.

Gilligan discovered that the attitudes of adult women toward competition are generally very similar to the attitudes that Lever found in young girls. Women place far more emphasis on relationships than on rules in making their moral judgments. Feelings of empathy and compassion are more influential than absolute principles. Women want to solve the *real* problems of how people are relating here and now.[27] Perhaps this approach to decision making fits the human service enterprises more accurately than the competitive approach of U.S. capitalism.

A summary formulation

Which human service strikes are most different from industrial strikes? Which cause the most serious ethical problems?

Perhaps the clearest way to answer these questions is to summarize the differences that we have discussed in this chapter in a simple formula. Four differences have emerged from this discussion that make us reflect most on the human service strike in a new way. Four adjectives express these differences.

1. Withdrawing a human service that is *client-centered* causes new and serious ethical considerations. What I am connoting by this term is that clients' needs are the dominant and all-encompassing reason for setting up the delivery system, e.g., in counseling or health care. The clients depend on no product, as in a coal strike or a public utilities strike. Since the client is the sole focus of the service and, in a sense, the only "object" involved, then the strike's pressure will always involve some inconvenience to the client.

2. Withdrawing a human service that is *directly delivered* to a client causes special ethical considerations. In this case, a human relationship develops between the worker and the client that is crucial to the service, e.g., in teaching, healing, or counseling. In the event of a strike, the worker is always confronted, not simply with theoretical questions about rights and duties, but with experiential questions about how the job action will touch these human relationships.

3. Withdrawing a human service that is in some way *necessary* for the client's well-being also causes special ethical considerations. This is the most subjective of the four characteristics. Some services seem necessary just because of a person's existence, e.g., health care for serious illness. Other services seem necessary because of how a particular society has developed, e.g., police protection and firefighting protection in large cities or education in a complex society.

Obviously, subjective judgments about "necessity" will be different, especially within the emotional context of a human service strike. When facing a particular strike, we must simply evaluate the actual circumstances of all the persons involved and their experiences to determine the service's degree of necessity.

4. Withdrawing a human service in a *not-for-profit* delivery system causes special ethical concern. The not-for-profit system was set up to address certain human needs in a community where those needs were not being met sufficiently. The continuing existence of such a system depends primarily on how effectively it meets the needs, not on its profitability. Decisions about the system will be made, or at least *should* be made, primarily on the basis of meeting needs, not on the basis of economics.

Because of this not-for-profit status, a special tension arises within management when a strike is threatened. Management presumes that most professional workers are involved in the system for the same reasons that management set it up, i.e., to supply the service. Most management personnel seem to think that a strike separates the workers from them in intentionality and that they are no longer of one mind in their motivation to deliver the service.

In a not-for-profit delivery system, everything in the collective bargaining process and in the strike somehow touches the delivery of the service. There is nothing else to touch: no profit, no concerns about possible future business investments, and no stockholders to please. Delivering the service is the pivotal point around which all other activity revolves.

The most serious ethical concerns therefore, arise in strikes involving *client-centered, directly delivered, necessary, and not-for-profit* human services.

Ethical classification of human services

Which human services fit within this summary description? The most accurate answer is that all belong, more or less, under one or more of the four considerations in the formula.

In making a practical application of the formulation, I presume that the more accurately a human service fits into all four considerations, the more serious are the ethical concerns when that human service is withdrawn. Most nurses, for example, use their skills in not-for-profit, client-centered institutions where they deal directly with patients. Their services are considered necessary, especially when they are working in emergency rooms, critical care units, or at nursing homes. Thus nurses' strikes usually raise serious ethical concerns.

Other human services may fit under only two or three of the headings, but their intensity and importance under those headings may raise ethical concerns as serious as those in the nursing example just mentioned. Police generally deal in not-for-profit, client-centered services, but forming client relationships (directly delivered) is often not as crucial as in health services or education. The necessity of their service is regarded as crucial, however, even more so than nurses dealing with common illnesses. Ordinary police service is regarded as urgent, especially in large cities, by almost everyone in society.

In the case of prison guards, relational skills are of lesser importance than they are to police working in a residential community.

The performance of their task, especially with violent criminals, is so necessary for the safety of society, however, that very serious ethical concerns arise if they threaten to withdraw their services.

Based on this kind of reflection on the summary formulation, I have attempted to categorize most human service workers in the chart at the end of this chapter. I selected three categories for the chart intuitively rather than scientifically; these categories seemed to be sufficient for indicating the actual differences that people have experienced in human service strikes.

I have purposely avoided using the categories proposed by some state legislatures, union officials, and political or legal theorists: "essential, semiessential, other."[28] In formulating these categories, their proponents seem to focus on only one of the characteristics in my summary formulation, i.e., the question of how *necessary* the service is. In their discussions of the meaning of "essential" or "necessary," most seem to concentrate on how much empirically verifiable harm would occur if the service were withdrawn: would anyone die, would people suffer permanent physical disabilities, would people be attacked by violent criminals, etc.

The criteria that I am suggesting, while affirming the importance of these concrete effects, also emphasize the *relational* effects of the withdrawal of human services. Influenced by the relationality-responsibility approach to ethics and the feminist psychological studies of researchers like Gilligan, I am suggesting that a focus solely on the concrete effects of actions is too narrow an approach for a genuinely human ethics. Perhaps the narrower approach is necessary in legal matters; legal justice demands empirical proof. In dealing with morality, however, the question of how our actions affect the total well-being of people is central. The quality of our human relationships is at the core of our human well-being.

An evaluation of human services in light of the four characteristics in the summary formulation leads to the following categorization of strikes by human service workers. (I judged that it would be too tedious to give a rationale for the classification of each group in the chart. I have simply evaluated each group as realistically as possible, trying to be faithful to the explanations of the four considerations). I have included in these categories workers who have, up to this point, rarely been organized into unions and have generally not taken part in job actions, e.g., psychologists, clergy. I have included them to be as comprehensive as possible and perhaps to anticipate the future.

Categories of Strikes According to Ethical Concerns

Strikes by:	*Lead to:*

A. Nurses
Physicians
Professional personnel
   at nursing homes
Counselors
Psychologists
Clergy
Psychiatrists
Police
Firefighters
Prison guards
Professional personnel
   at correctional
   institutions
Professional personnel
   at institutions for the
   handicapped or
   mentally ill
	A. Very serious
	   ethical concerns

B. Teachers (all levels)
Sanitation workers
Parole officers
Public utilities workers
Social workers
Child care workers
Health care workers
   with technical skills
   (physical therapists,
   occupational
   therapists,
   respiratory therapists
   x-ray technicians, etc.)
Orderlies and nurses'
   aides
Paramedics
	B. Some important
	   ethical concerns

Strikes by:	*Lead to:*

C. Postal workers
   Public transportation
   workers (airlines,
   bus, railways)
   Support personnel in
   health care,
   education,
   government (medical
   records, admissions,
   business office, etc.)
	C. Some lesser
	   (often indirect)
	   ethical concerns

Notes

1. For a detailed, eyewitness account of what "strikebreaking" connoted in that angry and violent confrontation, see Arthur Burgoyne, *The Homestead Strike of 1892* (Pittsburgh: University of Pittsburgh Press, 1979).

2. Charles Cogen, "Collective Negotiations in Public Education," in R.E. Walsh, ed., *Sorry...No Government Today* (Boston: Beacon Press, 1969), p. 144.

3. Cogen, p. 144.

4. Jack Barbash, *Union Philosophy and the Professional* (unpublished paper for the Department of Labor Studies, Pennsylvania State University, 1978), pp. 1-2.

5. Harvey L. Friedman, "The Role of the AFL-CIO in the Growth of Public Sector Collective Bargaining," in R.E. Walsh, ed., *Sorry...No Government Today* (Boston: Beacon Press, 1969), p. 29.

6. Arthur M. Ross and Paul T. Hartman, *Changing Patterns of Industrial Conflict* (New York: John Wiley & Sons, Inc., 1960), pp. 166-167.

7. Martin Tolchin, "Influence of the Profit Motive is Argued as Public Hospitals Turn to Chains," *The New York Times* (Jan. 26, 1985), p. A8; Linda B. Miller, "For-Profit Hospitals: What About the Poor?" *Washington Post* (Jan. 30, 1985), p. A19; Arnold S. Relman, "Investor-Owned Hospitals and Health Care Costs," *The New England Journal of Medicine* 309 (Aug. 11, 1983), pp. 370-372.

8. R.V. Pattison and H.M. Katz, "Investor-Owned and Not-for-Profit Hospitals," *The New England Journal of Medicine* 309 (Aug. 11, 1983), pp. 350-351.

9. Miller, p. A19.

10. Norman Metzger, Joseph M. Ferentino, and Kenneth F. Kruger, *When Health Care Employees Strike* (Rockville, MD: Aspen Systems Corp., 1984), p. 143.

11. Barbash, p. 2.

12. See Frederick H. Harbison, "Collective Bargaining and American Capitalism," in A. Kornhauser, R. Dubin, and A. Ross, eds., *Industrial Conflict* (New York: McGraw-Hill, 1954), pp. 270-276, for a tidy summary of the structure and goals of the collective bargaining process in U.S. industry.

13. In the case of police strikes, the motivation for some police working while others strike is usually more complex (because of the promotion system, ambiguity about whether different rankings make one part of management or labor, etc.) than the motivation of other human service workers, according to the study of five police strikes done by William D. Gentel and Martha L. Handman, *Police Strikes: Causes and Prevention* (Washington, DC: International Association of Chiefs of Police, Inc., 1979).

14. Ross and Hartman, pp. 2-3.

15. Anthony Cresswell, "Due Process in the Faith Community," *Origins* 6:34 (Feb. 10, 1977), p. 543.

16. Arthur Kornhauser, Robert Dubin, and Arthur Ross, "Alternative Roads Ahead," in *Industrial Conflict*, p. 512.

17. Metzger, Ferentino, and Kruger, pp. 96-97.

18. Legislative Research Bureau, State of Massachusetts, "The Right to Strike," in R.E. Walsh, ed., *Sorry...No Government Today* (Boston: Beacon Press, 1969), p. 237.

19. Legislative Research Bureau, p. 237.

20. *The National Labor Relations Board v. Yeshiva* (1980), no. 75-857.

21. AFL-CIO Committee on the Evolution of Work, *The Changing Situation of Workers and Their Unions* (AFL-CIO Department of Information, 1985), p. 13.

22. Many of my colleagues in economics insist that the U.S. system should be called a "modified free enterprise" system.

23. Henri Nouwen, *Creative Ministry* (New York: Doubleday Image Book, 1978), p. 6.

24. AFL-CIO Committee, p. 14.

25. AFL-CIO Committee, p. 15.

26. Carol Gilligan, *In A Different Voice* (Cambridge, MA: Harvard University Press, 1982), pp. 9-11.

27. Gilligan, pp. 69, 105.

28. These three categories appear in Statute #23.40.200 (1972) from the state legislature of Alaska. This law forbids strikes entirely by essential employees: police, fire protection employees, employees of jails, prisons, and other correctional institutions, and hospital employees.

The statute gives semiessential employees (utility, snow removal, sanitation, public school, other educational institution employees) the right to strike after mediation on approval by a majority of the bargaining unit until the work stoppage has begun to threaten the health, safety, or welfare of the public. Nonessential employees (all other public employees) have an unqualified right to strike if a majority of the bargaining unit approves. For other attempts at categorizing service workers according to these categories, see "A New Approach to Strikes in Public Employment," "Where One Union Stands," and "The Right to Strike," in R.E. Walsh, ed., *Sorry... No Government Today* (Boston: Beacon Press, 1969), pp. 68-69, 236, 243-250.

These authors agree that police, firefighters, and prison guards are essential. The categorization of health care employees varies from essential to semiessential. Teachers, sanitation workers, public utilities workers, and public transit workers are generally classified as semiessential, but one commentator allows that in certain circumstances they are all essential.

Part II

The Moral Considerations

Introduction

The very nature of morality and ethics is to attempt to determine the rightness or wrongness of human actions. But why are human beings so interested in making such determinations? What is the purpose of going through that sometimes painful process? What is to be gained from it? A traditional Christianity often answered this question by stating that to discover what was right and wrong was to discover God's will. If we followed God's will, we would receive an eternal reward in the end. Thus morality was often viewed as a collection of divine commands which, if obeyed, led to heaven.

There is basic truth in this traditional moral position. From the discussion of ethics and moral theology in Chapter One, however, it should be clear that many modern theologians would find this simplistic answer incomplete as well as misdirected. It tends to steer us away from more immediate and important concerns.

In a relationality-responsibility approach to morality, the primary reason for trying to decide if an action is right or wrong is to discover how to live life most fully. The goal of moral decision making is to lead human beings and society to their fullest possible development. Since, as we discussed before, the God who created us to be human is the same God who spoke to us in Christian revelation, to live in a fully human way is to live divinely. To become fully human and to become God-like are exactly the same thing.

The question about service strikes in the following chapters, "Are they right or wrong?" could be worded in a more challenging way: "Do strikes sometimes help human service workers and their clients, as well as management personnel, to come to their fullest human development?" We are seeking to discover if the pressure tactic of striking is sometimes a valuable means to bring everyone involved, and the delivery system itself, to a stage of development that they would not otherwise attain.

One other facet of traditional Christian morality should be clarified before discussing the morality of service strikes. Traditionally, many Christians have, consciously or unconsciously, thought of their morality as "a set of rules." Christians, as well as other religionists, would often refer to their moral tradition as "a moral code." This popular perception of morality led one to believe that one could discover if an action were right or wrong by going to the rulebook and finding the rule that applied to the action that one was considering.

The most appealing idea in this approach was that answers to moral questions were clear-cut. Often Christian moralists could respond to complex questions with a final "yes" or "no." Once again, from the discussion in Chapter One, it is obvious that a modern approach to morality goes beyond simple rule making and rule following.

Many modern moral theologians, especially those who take a relationality-responsibility approach, maintain that it is more realistic to conceive of the moral theologian as one *who guides people through the process of moral decision making* rather than as one who gives people the final answers. The science of moral theology can reveal the key issues that must be faced in making a moral decision about an action. Moral theology can challenge people to confront *all* the crucial questions about any decision. It can attempt to ensure that people who are making the decisions do not simply choose to consider those arguments that will support their already existing bias.

My purpose in these chapters is *not* to give a set of rules or absolute answers to all questions about human service strikes. Rather, my goal is to bring into focus the major considerations that persons involved in human service strikes must face in order to decide if they are acting morally. I then draw some conclusions about how I would evaluate these considerations.

The considerations enumerated here have surfaced consistently in my interviews with numerous representatives on both sides and in the literature on the topic. I am suggesting, therefore, that anyone who wishes to make an authentic moral decision about human service strikes must confront these issues and carefully figure out a response to them.

The four principal ethical issues involved in human service strikes are the following: *self-love* on the part of the workers; the sharing of *power* by everyone involved in the delivery of human services; the *rights* of everyone involved; and the question of *harm* to the client and to the delivery system.

The first two issues are concerned with the positive question of morality: Do human service strikes sometimes lead people and society to full human development? Do they enhance the self-love and assertiveness of workers that is crucial for being a mature human being? Do they help to give workers, clients, and management personnel a sense of power and freedom that makes everyone involved in the delivery of human services more responsible and more authentic?

The third issue, the question of rights, deals with both the positive and the negative dimensions of morality. Do strikes enhance the rights of workers who have been frustrated in the exercise of their rights and lead them to greater human fulfillment? On the other hand, do strikes take away clients' rights to health, education, and public safety and thereby impede their human fulfillment?

The fourth issue deals with the negative question of morality: Do human service strikes sometimes interfere with, damage, or permanently destroy part of clients' human growth or the community's well-being? Do they interfere with, damage, or permanently destroy the workers' relationships with clients, management personnel, and some of their fellow workers and thereby disrupt delivery systems that contribute to the fulfillment of the entire community?

Note how all four of these concerns have been significant in the three great liberation movements of the last half of the twentieth century: the women's movement, the black revolution, and the Third World liberation movement. The agents of these movements do not wish to do permanent harm to the "other side" (men, whites, the wealthy and powerful in the First and Second World). They are set, however, on pursuing those dimensions of human development—self-love, power, freedom, and rights—that will allow them to grow as equals in the world community. Perhaps it is no coincidence that, in any movement toward freedom and human development, the same tensions necessarily arise.

These same tensions may arise because in every freedom movement the goals are ultimately the same. As Dr. Martin Luther King, Jr., observed, the struggle for equality is never to be viewed as a battle with a victor and a vanquished. Rather, it is a struggle to unite all conflicting parties in a common bond of loving concern and to evoke a mutual understanding that allows everyone to grow side-by-side to the fullness of humanity that God wants for all creatures.[1]

Note

1.   Martin Luther King, Jr., *Stride Towards Freedom* (New York: Harper & Row, 1958), pp. 219-220.

Chapter 4

Love of Self

Manipulation to subservience

Unfortunately, in the Christian tradition, people were often made to feel guilty if they were concerned about themselves. Christian teachers created a popular consciousness which maintained that "to put oneself last" was the height of virtue. Phrases such as "don't step out ahead of others," "turn the other cheek," "don't be concerned if others take advantage of you," and "God first, others second, yourself last" were considered expressions of the perfect Christian attitude.[1] As we shall see shortly, such a position is contested, not just by contemporary theologians and psychologists, but by most of the theological tradition of ancient, medieval, and modern Christianity.

A misinterpretation of "meekness" in both the Old and New Testaments provided a further basis for encouraging Christians to allow themselves to be manipulated into positions of subservience. When the author of the gospel of Matthew states, "Blessed are the meek, for they shall inherit the earth" (Mt 5:5), he is *not* encouraging his followers to be meek. Rather, he is explaining what will happen to the meek.

As some modern theologians put it, Jesus is giving us "charter statements" in this section of the Gospel known popularly as the beatitudes.[2] The evangelist is not encouraging people to be "poor," "meek," "abused and persecuted" (Mt 5:3, 5, 11). He is simply giving encouragement to such people by pointing out how Jesus, the savior, will be on their side and will see to it that they have a just reward despite their present oppression.

Our understanding of what the New Testament values in the meek is clarified even more by contemporary Old Testament scholars. The group of people designated as "meek" were those who were faithful to Yahweh despite being oppressed. They were praised "not because they groveled in the dust of oppression, but because they tenaciously kept their eyes towards God," even in the worst of moments.[3] In the New Testament, these same people are praised for their persistence, not for their timidity.

The traditional Christian teaching on self-renunciation seemed to give a strong foundation for maintaining that good Christians should not think about themselves. The gospel message tells us so clearly: "If anyone would come after me, let that person deny self... whoever would save one's life will lose it, and whoever loses one's life for my sake will find it" (Mt 16:24-25). Does this passage teach that we should not care about ourselves at all and should lose all self-concern? The passage can only have such a meaning if we read the words literally, without considering their first-century context.

Like all the founders of the great religions, Jesus presumed that people were pursuing false goals and empty desires because they were not focusing clearly on what God intended. Without the divine message, people tend to pursue a "false self," i.e., goals that will not really bring them to fulfillment.[4] Jesus does not suggest that we destroy the self that was created by God. Rather, Jesus' teaching proclaims in paradoxical fashion that what most human beings in the first century AD were striving for would lead them away from human fulfillment and from union with the divine. In order to arrive at self-realization and a relationship with God, people would have to "deny" and "lose" that false and deluded self.

Modern psychoanalyst Erich Fromm comes to similar conclusions about the pursuit of the real self and the false self from his research into human behavior (his conclusions are especially interesting since he is not a theist). Fromm suggests that being "too self-centered" is not the primary problem of people in the twentieth century. Rather, their problem is that they do not know what to be self-centered about.

Fromm contends that we tend to seek goals and objects that will not really advance our development. We simply are not clear about what is genuinely good for our human growth. "The failure of modern culture lies not in its principle of... the pursuit of self-interest, but in the deterioration of the meaning of self-interest; not in the fact that people are too much concerned with their self-interest, but that they are not concerned enough with the interest of their real self; not in the fact that they are too selfish, but that they do not love themselves."[5]

Finally, women have especially been manipulated in the Christian tradition into thinking that they would be selfish, evil creatures if they were to think about their own needs. Jesus says nothing in the Gospels to create such an impression, but the Pauline letters have much in them to foster such a mentality. "Let a woman learn in silence with all submissiveness. I permit no woman to teach or to have authority over men" (I Ti 2:11-12). Paul himself writes in his first letter to the church at Corinth that if women "have anything they desire to know, let them ask their husbands at home. For it is shameful for a woman to speak in church" (I Co 14:35).

There is no doubt in the Christian tradition that the Pauline attitude about the submissiveness of women won out over the liberating attitude of Jesus. Feminist Madonna Kolbenschlag summarizes the socialization of women through history:

> [T]he female child is destined from her earliest years to learn how to exist for others.... This role will school her in self-forgetfulness, service and sacrifice, in nurturing rather than initiating behaviors. Above all, it will teach her to... wait, forever if necessary, for the expected *other* who will make her life meaningful and fulfilled. She will give up everything when the expected one comes, even the right of creating her own self. Whether it is a husband, a religion or a revolution, she is ready to live outside of herself, to abdicate from responsibility for herself in favor of something or someone else.[6]

Theologian Judith Plaskow draws a challenging conclusion from the fact that women have been socialized to gain their identity from others. She argues that they have been thereby led into sin! It is directly contrary to God's will in creation not to develop that precious piece of creation called "self." "The 'sin' encouraged by women's situation... is precisely the failure to become a self, the failure to venture into responsible self-creation."[7]

In this atmosphere of popular but not theologically sound Christian consciousness about self-love, human service workers, most of whom have been women, are easily manipulated into thinking that it is pure selfishness to consider their own needs. They are made to feel that the pursuit of their own needs by means of a work stoppage would be the ultimate act of self-centeredness, the ultimate negation of the command to love one's neighbor.

Owners and managers of religious and not-for-profit institutions tell social workers, nurses, and health care personnel that "unionizing means that you care more about yourselves than about your clients." Union leader Jerry Wurf complains that efforts by service workers "to improve wages and working conditions have been regarded as arrogant and unbridled self-interest and treated in a manner more appropriate to major insurrections," even though their wages and working conditions are often far inferior to those of their counterparts in profit-making industries.[8]

Teachers are challenged with the cry, "Think of the children!" when a strike threatens, implying that they would manifest no concern for their students by striking. Union leader David Selden counters with the response that it might sometimes be more harmful to the children not to strike. He questions whether it is "better for a child to lose a few days or weeks of schooling now than go through life handicapped by years of inferior education."[9]

In each of these instances the implication is that human service workers would be wrong to think about themselves and care about their own needs. Once they have chosen to work in a helping profession, they forfeit the right to pursue self-benefit. The popular Christian spirituality which seemed to extol submissiveness and not caring for self supported such an approach to human service workers. One government mediator whom I interviewed observed that, because people with the vow of poverty performed so many human services in previous centuries, the public was accustomed to thinking of teachers, social workers, etc., as people who should not care about their own advancement.

This popular Christian consciousness and the consequent mentality of the general public in the United States come from a misinterpretation of the teaching of Jesus and does not give a sound basis for analyzing the ethical issues involved in human service strikes. For an accurate understanding of the role of service workers in our society and for a fair ethical evaluation of strikes they are involved in, it is necessary to reevaluate this traditional distaste for self-love and discover what is sound Christian teaching about our relationship with our own persons.

The nature of Christian self-love

Self-love is and always has been a Christian virtue. In spite of the contrary attitude proposed by popular spirituality, there has been a constant teaching in the Christian tradition, sometimes contested and variously interpreted, that it is good for human beings to be concerned about their own needs, to pursue their own authentic advancement and self-development. Naturally much argument has surrounded what "authentic advancement and self-development" mean. I will attempt to clarify this phrase by looking to various analyses of it by some outstanding thinkers in the Christian tradition.

In Hebrew Scriptures the creation story in the first chapter of Genesis states that God created man and woman in the divine image (Gen 1:27). The author tells us, in a charming anthropomorphic way, that God looked at the divine accomplishments of the sixth day and found them to be very, very good (Gen 1:31).

All Jewish and Christian believers begin their understanding of their relationship to self, therefore, with the conviction that every human being, including self, is good because we all have an image of the divine within ourselves. Every human being reflects something of what God is like. Original sin did not destroy this divine dimension within human beings but simply made it more difficult for people to discover and nurture this sharing in divinity.

How should we respond to knowing that we resemble somewhat the infinite God? We should be very attracted to ourselves and should be willing to affirm, without embarrassment, what a good job God did in making us. Accurate self-knowledge leads us to understand more and more clearly how our intelligence, freedom, feelings, and instincts are similar to the qualities of our divine model. No wonder Augustine concludes that we should unhesitatingly "...love that which God made" *(Enarr. in Psalmis,* 18[2]14).

To discover the goodness and the talents within oneself is not vanity or self-indulgence; it is simply recognizing God's handiwork. To love self is to praise God.[10] When any of us, including human service workers, seek to develop the divine talents within ourselves, we are setting about a task that God intended. As one modern theologian has wisely pointed out, however, "We do not need a command to tell us to do what comes naturally, but we do need instruction to tell us how to do it properly."[11]

The second part of Jesus' love command in the Gospels seems to follow logically from this understanding of the creation story. He tells us: "You shall love your neighbor as yourself" (Mt 22:39;

Mk 12:31). According to modern scholarship, we should take this command literally, i.e., by loving ourselves we discover *how* to love our neighbors. By the very fact that we are in touch with ourselves first, we have the opportunity to discover divine goodness first within ourselves. The practice of self-love is the training ground for learning to love others.

Thirteenth-century philosopher-theologian Thomas Aquinas summarizes what it means to call self-love the "norm for loving our neighbors." This summary may still apply to twentieth-century people. How do we love ourselves? First, we are attracted to and have concern for ourselves because we discover divine reflections within ourselves. We are thereby prompted to look to find the divine image in our neighbors, confident that such an image is there. Therefore we wish only good for ourselves, never evil or destruction, and consequently wish only good for our neighbors. Finally, we are able to affirm and rejoice in and love ourselves not because we obtain pleasure or material gain from our love, but because we are good in ourselves. We can love our neighbors just because they are divine reflections and not simply because we obtain pleasure or material benefit from our love.[12]

Our theology of the goodness of all creation and our understanding of the second love command lead to an important conclusion regarding *how much* we should love ourselves in relation to our neighbors. Should we always love our neighbors more than ourselves? Even though both self-love and love for neighbor are excellent human acts, cannot we still argue that Christ's general teaching of unselfishness means that love for neighbor always comes first?

A practical answer to this question is "no." If the Christian interpretation of love discussed thus far is accurate, then we must conclude that self-love and love for neighbor are *equally* good actions. All of us, by virtue of creation, are equally valuable in the sight of God; we are all images of the divine. There is no reason to suggest that, by virtue of being "I," I am always second to "you." The "I" and "you" are, all other things being equal, indistinguishably valuable in the divine schema of reality.[13]

One further philosophical refinement on this notion of self-love is valuable for understanding the dynamic of human service strikes. If we genuinely love our neighbors as ourselves and attempt to do so with perfect equality, then we will seek to instill in our neighbors a self-love similar to our own.[14] Once we experience the value of self-love, we can only wish to share it if we are authentic Christians. Thus in any situation where conflict seems to exist between self-love and love for neighbor, one practical guide to resolving the conflict can be the intention to effect a result in which everyone involved will be able to love and respect themselves. All people then will know that their needs were considered and will perceive that they are important in the process, even if they did not get their immediate needs fulfilled.

Philosopher Martin D'Arcy makes this same point with admirable simplicity: "In every unity or whole, the part loves itself truly when it loves itself as a part and not as a separate individual."[15] This attitude is a sound practical guide for going about the task of loving self honestly and authentically. No one exists in isolation from the rest of the human community. We all affect one another in many ways by our personal decisions. We cannot love ourselves authentically if we are not conscious of the inescapable fact that each of us is part of a family, a local community, etc.

Consequently, we have a duty to acknowledge our self-growth and to develop our talents fully so that both we and the community come to full fruition; "...the realization of a good community, which is the moral concern of us all, is impossible on any other terms."[16] Only if every individual in the community has a genuine concern for self will the community prosper. Theologian Paul Ramsey reasons that every person has a vocation that is inextricably bound up with self-progress and community progress: "...as part of vocational service grounded in Christian love for neighbor, individuals have great responsibility for the development and use of all their natural capacities, or else they take responsibility for rashly throwing them away."[17]

At this point, the negative side (the dehumanizing, disintegrating, or sinful dimension) of self-centeredness should be fairly clear. Concern for self becomes wrong when carried out in isolation from other human beings and from God. When our vision rests solely on ourselves, as though we were not connected to others in the very roots of our existence, we begin to develop the warped perspective that makes us less than human. Self-centeredness, in this negative sense, means that we focus so much on self that we either do not notice or do not care to notice how all our decisions about self affect the communities of which we are a part. In modern analyses of human love, Christian theologians express this negative dimension of self-centeredness simply and accurately when they tell us that "self-love" becomes a caricature of itself when human beings "claim independence *over against* God"[18] and when they act as though they exist "independently of all other beings."[19]

Another term used by contemporary philosophers and psychologists helps to describe the experience of authentic self-love more fully: self-affirmation.[20] The term needs little explanation. When persons are conscious of their innate goodness, they should feel free to express it in order to understand it more fully. One should let it shine occasionally "on the hill top" and not hide it "under a bushel basket" (Mt 5:14-16).

Everyone needs to be affirmed. Everyone needs to be told about his or her good qualities, his or her good use of talents, etc. Why should anything be wrong with our doing this service for ourselves occasionally, just as we do it for others? As long as what we are affirming is true and we recognize the interrelatedness of our goodness to the divine and to others, then we act in a healthy way.

To prevent giving the impression that all Christian tradition has agreed with the theory of self-love proposed thus far in this chapter, I should mention the strongly opposing view of Reformation leader Martin Luther, a view affirmed by some Neo-Orthodox Protestant theologians today. Luther maintained that human nature is so corrupted by sin and so far astray from its original integrity at creation that it is utterly incapable of pursuing self-love without becoming self-centered in the worst sense of the term.[21] He looked with great pessimism at the results of self-love in the past and saw it causing only greed, hostility, and alienation from God and neighbors.

Admittedly I am taking a much more optimistic view of human nature in this study, a view that has been present in much of the Christian tradition. I *state* the view and describe it, rather than trying to *prove* it conclusively either theologically or philosophically. I appeal to the experience of each reader to verify that it fits human reality more accurately than its opposite.

Self-love and assertiveness

Modern psychology's emphasis on "assertiveness" as a primary means of developing a mature, well-integrated personality has helped theologians and philosophers understand Christian self-love more experientially. A brief look at the contemporary psychology of assertiveness reveals that, properly understood, it is simply self-love in action.

To be assertive means to identify one's own rights and the rights of others and then accept both. One is willing to admit without timidity that he or she does indeed have certain rights and is willing to articulate them and act on them while at the same time recognizing and respecting the rights of others.[22]

In popular language, assertiveness means a willingness to "stand up for one's own rights," without implying the brashness or hostility that the popular phrase often implies. The basic message of assertion is simple: "This is what I think. This is what I feel. This is how I see the situation. This message expresses 'who the person is' and is said without dominating, humiliating, or degrading the other person."[23] The assertive person seeks to be honest and straightforward without being apologetic or demeaning of self.

Included in this recognition of mutual rights is an assumption also present in the analysis of authentic self-love, i.e., one has no reason to presume that another person's rights are always more important than one's own. "We all have the right to have needs and to have these needs be as important as other people's needs . . . we have the right to ask . . . that other people respond to our needs and to decide whether we will take care of other people's needs."[24]

Popular Christianity taught an attitude that the rights of others were always more important than one's own and that the "Christian way to behave" was to defer to the rights of others first. As noted previously, such an attitude seemed to disregard the fundamental tenet of faith that *we* are good creatures of God just as much as *others*; we are endowed with the same rights by the divinity as everyone else. A sound theory of assertiveness does not recommend placing our needs first or treating the rights of others lightly. It does recommend, as does a sound theory of self-love, that we face daily reality with the presupposition that my rights and your rights are equally important and that the specific circumstances of the actual situation will decide whose rights have priority in the event of an irresolvable conflict.

A primary goal of assertive conduct is good communication. Assertive persons want to make sure that there is nothing false about the way they are relating with others. Implicit in this desire for authentic communication is the hope that the people with whom one is relating will also become more assertive and say truthfully how they feel and what they want from the relationship. "The goal of assertion is communication and 'mutuality', that is, to get and give respect, to ask for fair play, and to leave room for compromise when the needs and rights of two people conflict."[25]

This facet of assertiveness is particularly applicable to human service workers. So much of their work is the working out of relationships. If nurses, teachers, physicians, police, etc., pretend to have no needs, act as though they do not need a salary, and show no concern for their own feelings, they will probably not have satisfying relationships with their clients. According to psychological researchers, "personal relationships become more authentic and satisfying when we share our honest reactions with other people and do not block others' sharing their reactions with us."[26] The best human service worker is the one who admits to feelings and needs, even when these sometimes may conflict with the feelings and needs of those whom they serve.

One of the first results of thoughtful assertiveness is an increase in self-confidence. Psychologists state that the control gained by assertiveness is primarily over *self*, not necessarily over *others*.[27] Assertiveness is not domination of others or oppression in any sense. It is the kind of confidence in one's own actions that allows one to be free to state the painful truth when necessary and to be sensitive and kind as well. Christian assertiveness allows one to choose how strong and confronting one wishes to be in any situation. "'Aren't there times when I will decide I do not wish to be assertive?'" you may ask. The answer is a definite 'yes', as long as you are making this choice knowing that you have the skills necessary to be assertive if you so desire."[28]

In his theory of nonviolent resistance, Martin Luther King, Jr., makes the same point, from a social action point of view, that psychologists have made. The first effect of nonviolent confrontation, King writes, is not immediately to change the hearts of the oppressors. "It first does something to the hearts and souls of those committed to it. It gives them new self-respect; it calls up resources of strength and courage that they did not know they had."[29] Strong and honest confrontation, in the midst of which one has a loving concern for the person(s) being confronted, can bring both parties to a greater awareness of reality and to a deeper realization of their own inner strength.

With an optimism supported by research data, psychologists Patricia Jakubowski and Arthur Lange conclude that "when we stand up for ourselves and express our honest feelings and thoughts in direct and appropriate ways, everyone usually benefits in the long run."[30] Most people tend to respect those who have the courage to say what they mean and tend to respond more honestly themselves in such a dialogue.

Contrasting assertiveness to *aggressiveness* and *nonassertion* clarifies our understanding of this positive psychological attitude. Aggression always involves some violation of the rights of others. Through aggression, people attempt to gain their own ends by disregarding or destroying the rights of those who stand in their way.[31] The strength of the assertive person does not come from the power to conquer other people. It comes from the ability to face and evaluate conflicting rights and to compromise in such a way that "neither person sacrifices basic integrity and both get some of their needs satisfied."[32] King makes the contrast between aggression and assertion even more dramatic when he demands that nonviolent (assertive) resisters love the persons whom they are confronting, even in the midst of the confrontation.

Nonassertion is the complete opposite of aggression. To be nonassertive is to violate one's own rights. The nonassertive person in effect, says, "I don't count—you can take advantage of me. My feelings don't matter—only yours do. My thoughts aren't important —yours are the only ones worth listening to. I'm nothing—you are superior."[33] Such a person is overly apologetic, willing to do anything to keep the peace and avoid conflict. Deep inside themselves, nonassertive persons negate that they are unique reflections of the divine and dignified human beings.

Leaders of service unions have maintained that strike threats are frequently nothing more or less than responsible assertive statements in impasse situations. To act differently would be to act without self-respect. In a classic statement in 1919, the leader of the National Federation of Post Office Clerks, Thomas Flaherty, said at their national convention: "I can conceive of circumstances when to refrain from striking would be cowardly. There are far worse things than a strike. One is supine submission to injustice.... There is a constitutional inhibition against involuntary servitude."[34]

The president of the American Federation of Teachers (AFT) in 1965, David Selden, challenged the general public to think of the growing assertiveness of elementary and secondary teachers in terms of their growing self-respect rather than in terms of greed and unconcerned self-aggrandizement. He suggested that it took far greater courage to confront lethargic school boards and rusty educational systems than to allow the status quo to remain untouched and unchallenged. He called on the public, school boards, and school superintendents to "be delighted when they have a group of educators who care enough about the schools and their own professional status to lay their jobs on the line in order to bring about improvements."[35]

In summary, it seems accurate to conclude that the assertiveness described by contemporary psychologists is Christian self-love in action. In the light of this analysis, are strikes by human service workers acts of assertion or acts of aggression? Are they based on narrow self-centeredness or on authentic self-love? The next section attempts to answer these fundamental ethical questions.

Specific application of self-love to service strikes

From the previous discussion of Christian self-love and assertiveness, I will fashion two principles to help determine the morality of strikes by human service workers. The next two chapters on the other major moral issues each give three more principles. *All eight principles must be used together* to make a sound judgment about the morality of strikes; each represents only one facet of the problem. To rely exclusively on one principle to draw a conclusion will almost always lead to an incorrect moral judgment. (Perhaps it would be helpful at this point for the reader to glance at all the principles in this chapter and Chapters Five and Six before continuing to read this present analysis.)

Some overlap naturally occurs in the three discussions of the major moral issues. So as not to be unduly repetitive, I will make all the major points about each issue under the proper heading. Thus, in this first discussion about the principles concerning self-love, I simply *state* that the principle holds "as long as no disproportionate harm is done to the clients" and leave a full explanation of "disproportionate harm" to Chapter Six.

Principle 1

Human service strikes are morally justified when they are the only means left to the workers to overcome the "manipulation to subservience" by management and by the public (as long as no disproportionate harm is done to the clients or to the delivery system in the process).

As previously stated, a popular attitude in contemporary Christianity has encouraged people never to think about their own needs and caused them to feel guilty if they were concerned about themselves. Often the general public and owners and managers of voluntary institutions have used this popular trend to manipulate service workers into passivity concerning their role in the delivery of human services. Teachers, nurses, social workers, and guidance counselors are subtly pressured to feel that they are greedy and not following their professional ideals if they become concerned about wages, working conditions, or even about their own creative methods for delivering their services.

A pervasive modern atmosphere is simply telling them, "Don't you dare love yourselves. Don't be so bold as to think that you should live on the same level as other workers in our society." This exhortation is obviously contrary to our theology of Christian self-love. It can hinder their growth as healthy individuals and gradually corrode their self-worth, consequently preventing the whole delivery system from reaching its full growth potential.

If all other efforts to overcome this manipulation have failed, then the pressure tactic of a strike could be a valid means for pursuing this Christian goal of authentic self-love. It is important to emphasize that all other means must have been reasonably pursued. This assertion leads to a challenging observation about the present practices of some unions. For some, "all other reasonable means" refers only to those developed in the field of industrial labor relations. Certain unions seem to presume that traditional collective bargaining, with its posturing and overstated proposals, is *the* means. The recent self-study of the AFL-CIO speaks critically of such a mentality when it states that collective bargaining should not be "confined by any rigid and narrow formula," as though the union movement had created an "orthodoxy" that everyone must now follow.[36]

Creative new ways of attempting to resolve differences between service workers and management have been and are being worked out, e.g., integrative bargaining and collective gaining (see Chapter Five for a discussion of these). These new methods assume that something is sufficiently different about human services to warrant a different approach to bargaining. I am pointing out here only that the statement, "all other means were tried," can have a broader meaning in the human services than it has had in profit-making industry.

Principle 2

In deciding whether or not to strike, human service workers are morally justified in putting their ordinary needs on the same level of importance as the ordinary needs of their clients.

"Ordinary needs" are those which everyone must have fulfilled in order to have a dignified life. Service workers and their clients have the same need to be treated with dignity, to receive a just wage, to have some stability in their employment, to know that their supervisors are treating them honestly, to have reasonable access to education and health care, to have reasonable assurance of protection from crime, etc.

If human service workers are being treated unjustly, i.e., if some of their ordinary needs are not being fulfilled, they have no reason to put their clients' ordinary needs *always* before their own. One of the most basic observations in the analysis of Christian self-love states that "we," "you," and "they" are equally valuable in the sight of God, that all have the same God-given rights and worth. Service workers who weigh their ordinary needs against those of their clients are behaving in a just and loving way.

If human service workers are being treated unjustly, and no other way is available to correct the injustice, they may choose to disrupt a delivery system that provides for their clients' ordinary needs. They would be dealing with equal factors, i.e., one set of ordinary needs against another set. They would be making a responsible decision to cause temporary disruption to the one in order to ensure a more permanent regard for the other.

To put this confrontation in the language used in our discussion of self-love, human-service workers striking would be viewing their needs in the "context of the whole system, of the whole community of which they are a part."[37] They would cause some inconvenience temporarily to one part of the system to bring about a more just functioning for another part, thereby enhancing the total system.

In popular language, they would cause some inconvenience but no permanent damage. To cause some inconvenience for the sake of their own self-development and for the sake of improving the whole system can be healthy, assertive behavior. To cause serious harm to clients, even in behalf of the two worthy goals of self-development and the improvement of the system, is another matter.

In philosophical language, risking serious harm to clients would ordinarily amount to workers' weighing their ordinary needs against the extraordinary (i.e., crucial, emergency) needs of their clients, an offense against the basic tenets of Christian love. They would be putting something less important about themselves (working conditions, wages) before something far more important to others (emergency surgery, a critical moment in the counseling process). They would be destroying something crucial in the lives of other people in the interest of obtaining something less crucial for their own development.

Striking human service workers must, therefore, make sure that their clients' extraordinary needs are being met. It has been encouraging to discover that nurses and police often have prepared for weeks or months before a strike to ensure that all such extraordinary needs would be met. In such cases, the management personnel who control the system experience greater disruption than the clients.

This second principle has emphasized that human service workers must constantly view their own needs within the context of the whole system and community of which they are a part. Viewing their needs in isolation, with no focus on their clients' needs or the delivery system's effectiveness, would be the kind of self-centeredness previously described as offensive to authentic Christian self-love.

Striking workers in profit-making industries have not been challenged to view "the whole system" in the same way as human service workers. The difference stems from the way that capitalism developed in the United States. The capitalist enterprise does not demand that one be carefully attentive to the impact that one's business investment will make on the whole political-social-personal community. Rather, the capitalist enterprise presumes, that if people invest their money wisely and honestly, everyone will eventually benefit. The important question in capitalism is: "What have I produced with the goods and talents God has given me?" and not "Have the goods that I have produced been well distributed for the benefit of all?"[38]

Capitalism also presumes that, if profits are up and the gross national product is increasing, everyone in the local and national community will eventually be "better off." Consequently, "to get as much as you can out of the system," to push to get "as much as the market will bear," is viewed as sound behavior in a capitalist system. In the "long run," everyone will benefit.

I am suggesting that, because industrial unions grew up within the capitalist system and absorbed the capitalist spirit, there is an immediate tension, often subtle and unconscious, with the spirit that pervades not-for-profit human service delivery systems. Human service systems do not operate on the presumption that everyone will be "better off" if the systems are functioning profitably and if everyone is getting as much as they can. The presumption here is that everyone will be better off (1) if all who need the service have access to it and (2) if the service is being delivered more and more effectively.

In applying this second principle, service unions must accept a certain responsibility for the needs of everyone involved in their delivery system, including themselves, if they wish to act ethically. No corresponding responsibility has existed for unions in the profit-making industries, at least not in the way these have developed inside U.S. capitalism.

Notes

1. Michael Emmons and David Richards, *The Assertive Christian* (Minneapolis: Winston Press, 1981), p. 3.

2. Timothy E. O'Connell, *Principles for a Catholic Morality* (New York: Seabury Press, 1978), p. 27.

3. Emmons and Richards, p. 47.

4. Emmons and Richards, p. 38.

5. Erich Fromm, *Man for Himself: An Inquiry into the Psychology of Ethics* (Greenwich, CT: Fawcett Premier, 1966), p. 143.

6. Madonna Kolbenschlag, *Kiss Sleeping Beauty Good-Bye* (New York: Bantam Books, 1979), pp. 9-10.

7. Judith Plaskow, *Sex, Sin and Grace* (Washington, DC: University Press of America, 1980), p. 114.

8. Jerry Wurf, "An Address to the Mayors," in R. E. Walsh, ed., *Sorry...No Government Today* (Boston: Beacon Press, 1969), p. 73.

9. David Selden, "Needed: More Teacher Strikes," in R. E. Walsh, ed., *Sorry...No Government Today* (Boston: Beacon Press, 1969), p. 113.

10. Martin D'Arcy, *The Mind and Heart of Love, Lion and Unicorn: A Study in Eros and Agape* (New York: Henry Holt & Co.), 1947, p. 92.

11. Oliver O'Donovan, *The Problem of Self-Love in St. Augustine* (New Haven, CT: Yale University Press, 1980), p. 56.

12. John J. Cain, *Self-Love and Self-Donation: A Study in Aquinas' Concept of Self-Love* (Hales Corners, WI: Priests of the Sacred Heart, 1976), pp. 76-77.

13. O'Donovan, pp. 143-144.

14. O'Donovan, p. 116.

15. D'Arcy, p. 91.

16. W.G. Maclagan, "Self and Others: A Defence of Altruism," *Philosophical Quarterly* 4 (April 1954), p. 119.

17. Paul Ramsey, *Basic Christian Ethics* (New York: Charles Scribner's Sons, 1950), p. 159.

18. Anders Nygren, *Agape and Eros*, trans. by Philip S. Watson (New York: Harper & Row, 1969), p. 649.

19. Cain, p. 63.

20. See Jules J. Toner, *The Experience of Love* (Washington, DC: Corpus Books, 1968), pp. 171-172, for a brief psychological explanation of the term.

21. For a clear summary of Luther's analysis of self-love, see Nygren, pp. 710-712; and Gene Outka, *Agape: An Ethical Analysis* (New Haven, CT: Yale University Press, 1972), pp. 58-60.

22. Arthur J. Lange and Patricia Jakubowski, *Responsible Assertive Behavior* (Champaign, IL: Research Press, 1976), p. 2.

23. Lange and Jakubowski, p. 7.

24. Lange and Jakubowski, p. 56.

25. Lange and Jakubowski, p. 8.

26. Lange and Jakubowski, p. 56; see also pp. 12-13.

27. Lange and Jakubowski, p. 13.

28. Emmons and Richards, p. 10.

29. Martin Luther King, Jr., *Stride Towards Freedom*, (New York: Harper & Row, 1958), p. 219.

30. Lange and Jakubowski, p. 55.

31. Lange and Jakubowski, pp. 38-39.

32. Lange and Jakubowski, pp. 8-9.

33. Lange and Jakubowski, p. 9.

34. Murray B. Nesbitt, *Labor Relations in the Federal Government Service* (Washington, DC: Bureau of National Affairs, Inc., 1976), pp. 365-366.

35. Selden, p. 112.

36. AFL-CIO Committee on the Evolution of Work, *The Changing Situation of Workers and Their Unions* (Washington, DC: AFL-CIO Publication No. 165, 1985), p. 15.

37. D'Arcy, p. 91.

38. See "Towards the Future: Catholic Social Thought and the U.S. Economy," *Catholicism in Crisis* 2:12 (November 1984), pp. 25-31, for a defense of this view of economics.

Chapter 5

Sharing of Power

Relationship of love, power, and freedom

Love of God, self, and neighbors is the essence of Christian life. If Christ's teachings command us to live a Christian life, we must have the *power* to carry out the precepts of love. To love necessitates having power; without it, a person has no real capacity to love. "The Christian goal of love of self and love of neighbour...can only be attained when a person first of all possesses the power to love."[1]

Psychoanalyst Rollo May maintains that we hesitate to connect power and love because we tend to think of power primarily as compulsion and love as a tender emotion. Both these descriptions are only part of the total reality of love and power. In agreement with modern theologians, May reasons that love and power are intimately related: "That power and love are interrelated is proved most of all by the fact that one must have power within oneself to be able to love in the first place."[2]

In the categories discussed in Chapter Four on self-love, the relationship between power and love would work out in the following way. Christian self-love guides us to have a concern for self within the framework of the whole community of which we are a part. We must weigh our own needs and those of our neighbors in the light of Christian teaching and make careful decisions about how to pursue these various needs so that the whole community will benefit most fully. Consequently, we must have some power to carry out our decisions. We must have some capacity to shape those realities that make up our social, occupational, and political communities.

Theologian Romano Guardini expresses this necessity of power in Christian life so boldly that some traditional Christians might feel uncomfortable with his statements. He maintains that the most fundamental (but not necessarily the most important) way that we reflect God is by sharing in divine power. If we are to think and act in a God-like way, we must share in the divine power to carry it out. Guardini writes that our "natural God-likeness consists in our capacity for power...the exercise of power is essential to our humanity."[3] Power is not a special gift for a select few; it is fundamental to the humanness of everyone.

Power is so fundamental for a sound human existence that people may be called mentally unhealthy without it. May insists that "a common characteristic of all mental patients is their powerlessness...an almost complete lack of capacity to influence or affect other people in interpersonal relations."[4] It may logically follow, then, that any society or system that has large numbers of powerless people within it is unhealthy as well. Another psychologist, Edgar Friedenberg, makes the same point as he revises the famous saying about power attributed to Lord Acton: "All weakness tends to corrupt, and impotence corrupts absolutely."[5]

This observation about power being foundational for our humanness leads to another striking conclusion, not usually associated with a Christian approach to life. Not only is it our right to seek power, but sometimes it is our duty. If we have a God-given duty to love and some external force prevents us from putting our love into action, we should seek to overcome that force with our own power. If we become convinced that certain needs are not being met that are crucial for the full development of one of our communities, then we have a duty to pursue the power necessary to meet those needs, even when the needs are our own. German theologian Karl Rahner concludes that a time comes in the lives of most people when they "have not merely the right, but...even the moral duty, of insisting on their respective rights."[6]

Philosophers, theologians, and psychologists make one final observation about power in Christian life that will be valuable for our understanding of the power tactic, the strike. Power is necessary for freedom. Without some power, no human being is truly free. If God created us to be free, then it follows that our Divine Source must want us also to be powerful, i.e., to be able to exercise our freedom. To be precise, the power necessary for freedom must have two dimensions to it. First, it must be characterized by an "inner force" that moves a person to act; and second, this force must be strong enough to overcome the external restrictions that would prevent it from arriving at its goals.[7] Rahner concisely expresses what is perhaps an obvious fact of life: "Power *exists*. And it rightly exists, because it is the condition of the possibility of freedom."[8]

As already seen in our study of the historical development of service strikes, it was the "frustration of powerlessness" that first led human service workers to use the strike as a pressure tactic in collective bargaining. They perceived that they had little or no influence over the delivery systems to which they have often committed their lives. They perceived that they had little or no control over the conditions of and compensation for their work. At the same time they saw industrial workers gaining more power and experiencing more freedom.

It is understandable *why* human service workers sought more power in their roles as public servants. Such a pursuit of power is a healthy human drive. We cannot glibly conclude, however, that *all* power leads to human fulfillment, and every pursuit of power is valuable human conduct. Some uses of power, especially violent uses, obviously can be very destructive to persons and values. Before we attempt to fashion any principles concerning the use of power in human service strikes, we must first examine two issues.

The first is the nature of authentic human power. How do we define and describe the power that builds up rather than destroys the human community? The second is the question of how to pursue power or seek some power sharing. After examining these issues, we should be able to see more clearly when and how the use of power in a strike does or does not lead authentically to human fulfillment for those involved.

To clarify our experiential understanding of the nature of power, we should review some of the reasons why the Christian tradition has had a fear of power and suspicion of people who seek power. By clearing away some misconceptions that lead to this negative feeling about power, we will be better prepared to examine the phenomenon of power in a positive human and Christian way.

Christian suspicion of power seeking

"Power tends to corrupt, and absolute power corrupts absolutely."[9] Perhaps no aphorism in the English language has caused greater suspicion of a human phenomenon than Lord Acton's description of the effects of power. If one accepts his account of power as accurate, then one naturally must seek to avoid it or at least accept it only grudgingly.

A friend of Friedrich Nietzsche, Jacob Burckhardt, gives another classic description of power that leads to the same negative feeling: "...power is of its nature evil, whoever wields it. It is not stability but a lust, and ipso facto insatiable, therefore unhappy in itself and doomed to make others unhappy."[10] If power is indeed a lustful desire that, once tasted, can never be satisfied, why would any right-minded human being seek it?

Chairman Mao-Tse-Tung, one of the most successful revolutionaries and power holders of the twentieth century, describes political power in terms so blatant that one could only conclude that it is inherently evil: "Political power grows out of the barrel of a gun."[11]

All these descriptions of power come from a conscious or unconscious perception of power as "brute force," or at least as the ability to manipulate others regardless of their real needs. Brute force and manipulation have been associated with power, but they are only a small part of the total experience.

James Hanigan summarizes this first reason for our negative feelings about power. Our misgivings come from "a confusion between violence and power," from a fear of "the possible coercive experience involved in many exercises of power and strength."[12] To overcome this fear, we need to understand clearly that violence or intrusiveness into the well-being of others does not necessarily belong to the nature of power. The following section on the nature of power clarifies this point.

A second reason why the Christian tradition has had a negative reaction to power seeking comes from its emphasis on the virtues of poverty and obedience as "evangelical counsels." Obedience implies giving one's power to another and trusting in the other to give sound direction to one's actions. Poverty, although interpreted in a score of different ways in the Christian past, generally implies the renouncing the pursuit of wealth, which is a chief means for achieving social and political power.[13]

One can see why people with vows of poverty and obedience would be thought of as virtuous but powerless. One can also see why society would consider it indecent of them to seek power. Power seeking would directly contradict the values that they seemed to be holding up as ideal in Christian life.

One federal mediator whom I interviewed made an incisive observation about the relationship of these vows to the unionization of, and right to strike by, human service workers. He maintained that society had become accustomed to receiving human services from people with religious vows and ideals and had grown to feel that such people needed little recompense or power in return for their services. If their life goal was to serve others, then let them do so without any consideration of their own status! Consequently, all human service workers could easily be made to feel guilty about pursuing power.

Hanigan gives another reason why Christians have erroneously felt uneasy with seeking power. He maintains that the Christian tradition has sometimes "sentimentalized" the conditions of human deprivation and powerlessness. In the Scriptures, the "lost sheep," "widows and orphans," "the crippled and the blind" are favorites of Jesus. He seeks them out. He wishes to be with them much more than with the wealthy and powerful. The Christian tradition gradually made them into heroes, into ideal people.[14] It is a short step to concluding that all Christians should imitate them.

Jesus does not hold up the powerless as examples to his followers. A careful examination of the Scriptures reveals that he attempts to empower them, to help them out of their misery, to teach them how to use power wisely and generously if they should attain it. A "romanticizing" of poverty, deprivation, and powerlessness in the Scriptures leads to a conclusion that is contrary to genuine Christian teaching, i.e., that living in powerlessness is good because God will take special care of you.

Finally, May suggests that all people of good will are suspicious of power seeking because of the way that our Western tradition has confused the relationship between power and love. "Love is seen as powerless and power as loveless. The more one develops a capacity for love, the less one is concerned about manipulation and other aspects of power. Power leads to domination and violence; love leads to equality and human well-being."[15]

As noted, May is convinced that this confusion comes from seeing love primarily as an emotion and power primarily as compulsion, a capacity to invade the domain of others. In this confused view, love is only soft and gentle, whereas power is always stern and demanding. Love always gives in to the beloved; power always gets its own way. This pattern of thinking is a jaundiced way of viewing two compatible human activities.

Love is often strong and demanding, as in the case of conscientious parents with their children. A person who loves seeks to render what is best for his or her beloved, and does not simply give in to what the beloved asks for. A person who loves seeks to enhance the dignity and the independence of the beloved and does not allow the beloved to hand over these precious qualities to anyone, not even to the lover.

If we view power and love as opposing one another, we usually would choose love over power. We would see power as a negative force in our lives that turns us into stern and unloving disciplinarians. May concludes that much of Western philosophical and theological tradition has viewed power as a negative or at least tainted dimension of social relationships. Power was either to be avoided completely or, at most, accepted with great reluctance. In our Western culture, power appears to be something that no self-respecting person should want. And, if put in the position of having to exercise it, a well-intentioned person should certainly not enjoy it.

The nature of power

Power is not an object that may be dissected and examined in a laboratory. Power is an experience, not a commodity. Any attempt to define or describe power is an attempt to articulate an experience. Perhaps the only way to tell if one has been successful in describing it is to ask if most people can identify with the description. If most respond, "Your definition and descriptions fit what I go through when I believe that I am exercising power," one may conclude that something meaningful has been said about the reality that society has chosen to name "power."

When attempting to define power, all learned disciplines are faced with the same challenge: to say something that fits human experience. Social psychology, philosophy, theology, political science, etc., have their special approaches to the definition and their own specific interests in determining what is most important about the experience. Theology's contribution always faces a special challenge from the more empirical disciplines because of its claim to some kind of divine communication (e.g., an experience of the spirit, biblical revelation). Even theology's claim to a special source of information about power, however, will be tested for its accuracy in the laboratory of common human experience.

Chapter One discusses the assertion from modern theologians that no essential difference exists between Christian morality and authentic human ethics. Good Christian actions are good human actions. It follows that a sound human description of power from any discipline will not differ from a theological description. The emphases and concerns may vary, but the final descriptions must be generally the same. (I say "generally" because every person may have a slightly different personal and individual experience of the phenomenon.)

What is power? Guardini says simply that it is "the ability to move reality."[16] It is an inner energy that makes people feel that they can change things, even in the face of resistance. Rahner adds that using this inner energy does not depend on the consent of others for its effectiveness, even if others are going to be affected and changed by its usage. He calls power "a certain self-assertion and resistance proper to a given being and . . . its innate possibility of acting spontaneously, without the previous consent of another, to interfere with and change the actual constitution of that other."[17] Just because the affected party's consent is not necessary when power is used, however, does *not* mean that no power is exercised when consent is given. It is far more accurate to conclude that power is exercised ideally when it evokes free consent from others and persuades and influences others so effectively that they freely join in its direction and impetus.

Max Weber emphasizes that all uses of power are in the context of social relationships; it never exists or is used in a vacuum. "Power is the probability that one actor within a social relationship will be in a position to carry out his (or her) own will despite resistance, regardless of the basis on which this probability rests."[18] "Social relationship" here should not be narrowly interpreted to mean "other human beings." The experience of power is actualized in any of the four great relationships that are a part of everyone's existence: to self, to other people, to material creation, and to the divine. Thus, people also act with power if they overcome laziness within themselves, if they overcome some force in the material world, or if they decide to relate in a new way with the divine.

In her discussion of power and violence, Hannah Arendt insists that all uses of human power must have purpose.[19] Accidents are not examples of "power." If a person unwittingly drops a heavy object on another person, neither party has been involved in a power relationship. It serves no useful purpose to call this incident an "act of power" just because it involves some physical force.

Finally, Paul Tillich's rather erudite description of power illustrates a practical facet of the human experience of power. Tillich writes that power is "being, actualizing itself over against the threat of non-being."[20] In this terse metaphysical language, he is pointing out simply that everything that comes into existence wishes to continue in existence. Everything, animate and inanimate, tends toward survival. Nothing that exists has nonexistence as its goal. Thus, the energies within human beings at birth instinctively tend to fight for continuing existence. Since *we are*, we wish to *continue to be*; an instinctive inner energy pushes us toward that goal.

The practical contribution of Tillich's definition of power for the study of human service strikes is simply to emphasize that the quest for power is both natural and essential for human beings to develop fully. The possessing of some degree of power is part of the definition of being human. The quest for some power is instinctive and humanizing.

From this assortment of descriptions of power from the various academic disciplines,[21] we discover five characteristics that provide a picture of power that should fit most people's experience:

1. Power is an inner energy that enables us to perceive that we can move reality.

2. Power is an inner energy that instinctively tends to keep its possessor in existence.

3. Power enables us to change realities that affect other people, even without their permission.

4. In human beings, power always has purpose.

5. Power is always exercised in the context of a social relationship (either to self, others, the material world, or the divine).

The use of power

In itself, power is neither good nor bad. Power is a necessary fact of human existence and can be used well or badly. It is good to have power, but all power is not necessarily good. In general, power is used well when regulated by the norms of love and justice.

As discussed earlier, love guides people in their use of power by ensuring that they pay attention to the needs of everyone in the community and make honest judgments about which needs demand immediate attention. Authentic love always sees self and others as parts of the whole community, never as isolated entities. Love guides people to weigh the needs of self and others equally in order to decide how best to promote the well-being of the whole community. Under the guidance of love, the use of power can never be arbitrary. Power is always directed toward the fulfillment, not the destruction, of people within their social relationships.

Justice tempers power in much the same way. Justice guides us to use power with great concern for others' rights as well as for our own. Justice demands that we weigh our own and others' rights and damage neither. Occasionally, we must decide which rights have priority and then pursue those, without directly or intentionally harming another's rights in the process.

Can a person who is just and loving use power to "compel" others to perform some action? Certainly. If a person has reasoned carefully about the needs and rights of all concerned and takes care not to trample these needs or rights of others, then sometimes forcing people to certain actions can be very just and loving. Tillich states this conclusion clearly: "What is the relation of justice to the compulsory element of power? The answer must be: it is not compulsion which is unjust, but a compulsion which destroys the object of compulsion instead of working towards its fulfillment."[22] If we compel people to achieve their own fulfillment, then we have acted justly.

Not all acts of power require compulsion. All acts of power do involve some inner energy, or strength, or forceful impact. At times, however, people may willingly accept the force imposed on them by another. In such cases, power has indeed been exercised. The power's impact has caused an effect on the respondent that may never have occurred if the power user had not acted. The respondent, however, was not "forced" to act in the sense of being compelled against one's will. The respondent freely joined in the strength of the original act to become part of its impetus. Such a sequence is not simply an example of a power act; it is an example of the *ideal* functioning of power.

Under the guidance of justice, people recognize that, as their power grows, so does their duty to use it well. All power implies duty, and in this sense, power is indeed a *burden*. The more power people have, the greater their responsibility to effect the growth of the whole community of which they are a part or over which they have some control. In a sound Christian tradition, all power has been connected to "service, common good, and the general interest."[23]

A slight revision of a maxim from medieval philosophy contrasts this just and loving use of power with a domineering and manipulative use. The authentic power user says, "I am in power and I command this action because it is just and beneficial." The arbitrary and domineering user of power says, "I am in power and this action is just and beneficial because I command it." The goodness of power actions comes from an honest evaluation of the acts based on the norms of love and justice, not from the arbitrary decisions of the one who happens to be in power.

In practice, it can be extremely difficult to determine if people are acting according to principle or expediency. Elizabeth Janeway presents an interesting challenge to self-examination for all power users: "The good names—capability, potentiality, creativity—aren't these just cover-ups for unpleasant instinctual drives which we use when power belongs to *us*? And what we describe as compulsion, domination, and oppression— aren't these pejoratives attached to power when we don't own it, when it's your power or their power?"[24]

Confident that human nature is not totally corrupt, I trust that such a rationalization is not always the case, although it is a common temptation. One can use no easy formula to determine if one's use of power is always authentic in actual practice. This practical uncertainty, however, in no way disproves the assertion that power, used justly and lovingly, leads to human fulfillment and should be pursued.

Biblical reflections on power

Jesus was very concerned about the use of power in first-century Palestine. Some of his comments reflect a different attitude from popular contemporary notions about the most important considerations regarding power. Those facets of Jesus' teaching on power that seem most pertinent to human service strikes are presented here and tested them in the same crucible used for all philosophical, psychological, and sociological comments—human experience. As noted in Chapter One, a distinctly Christian ethic different from human ethics, does not exist. If Jesus' teachings fit reality, then they should be valuable for describing any human being's experience and helpful to anyone who wishes to make a moral judgment.

Jesus was an advocate for the powerless.[25] In his Sermon on the Mount, he promises divine rewards to the meek, the poor, and the dispossessed. He regularly sought the company of those who were on the bottom rung of society's ladder: lepers, prostitutes, tax collectors, the crippled, and the blind. He did everything he could to make them "feel at home" with him.

He never blessed their powerlessness, he never encouraged them to remain in their deprived state. Instead he promised that, when the "reign of God" came to earth, they would be in power. He manifested to all who heard his word that he had come to empower the powerless. From a Christian perspective, therefore, one of the first concerns in the use of power is to discover how to share that power with those who traditionally have been powerless. Power sharing, not power preserving, is Jesus' central concern.

Second, Jesus was very critical of the way that those in authority used their power. He accused the powerful of using their position and prestige to manipulate the poor and the dispossessed. He accused them of domination and oppression.[26] He insisted that, when the "reign of God" was established, those in power would no longer lord it over their subordinates. "This must not happen with you. No, the greatest among you must behave...as if they were the ones who serve....I am among you as one who serves!" (Lk 22:26-27).

Jesus emphasized that power is service rather than oppression or domination. We must take care, however, not to interpret "service" as something weak and completely self-effacing. In the contemporary use of language one may think of a "doormat" personality when thinking of the one who serves.

Service does not imply weakness or timidity. In order to serve, one must have the power to serve.[27] Jesus speaks against that kind of power use that would keep the lowly in their position of subjugation. He speaks in favor of a power that would empower the lowly and strain to serve everyone equitably.

Service should imply that the people doing it have confidence that they know something about the correct way to approach their task. They should be willing to press for being able to carry out their work according to their own ideals.

Third, Jesus teaches that the power of love is the greatest force in the world. Nothing stronger or more influential exists. Consequently, loving action should be the final and most forceful "weapon" for Christians, not physical violence.[28] Loving action can be forceful, but it can never be destructive. Significantly, no New Testament author ever uses the Greek term for "brute force" (kratos) when speaking of Jesus' power, or records that Jesus ever used that term for power.[29] It is the exact opposite of the "love force" that Jesus preached.

Note how well these three biblical characteristics of power use fit power in human service work. Every human service in some way intends to empower needy clients; the power involved here is, by definition, service; and human services are most effective when they are delivered lovingly.

Categories of power according to sources

In the past three decades social psychologists have fashioned some useful categories for understanding the various kinds of power. They have attempted to describe human experience by focusing on the different ways that people come to possess power and typically use power. Since contemporary theology sees "common human experience" as one of the two basic sources for theology (the other being the sacred texts of religious tradition) this study may gain some valuable insight from investigating these categories of power.

Social psychologists Bertram Raven and John French, in a study published in 1959, suggested that people experience five different kinds of power in their human relationships.[30] These five categories come from an analysis of the sources of power, not specifically from the *uses* of power (another grouping reviewed next). French and Raven ask the questions: Why do certain people have power? What are its sources? On what foundations has their power been established? I will review the five categories briefly and then suggest that three of them may be helpful in understanding the power conflict between management and human service workers.

The first is *reward power*, defined simply as "power whose basis is the ability to reward."[31] If John recognizes that Frances* can mediate a reward, and John has a strong desire for the reward, then Frances has some significant power over John.

The second is *coercive power*, whereby John recognizes that Frances can punish him if he refuses to accept the influence or compulsion that she is attempting to exercise. Because of the ability to punish, Frances has significant control over John.[32]

The third category, according to the authors, is the most complex. *Legitimate power* is that power which "stems from internalized values in John which dictate that Frances has a legitimate right to influence him and that he has an obligation to accept this influence."[33] In this case, John, because of values that have been taught by parents, religious tradition, schooling, or some other influential source, feels that he "should" obey—indeed "must" obey—or else be guilty of a betrayal of those values. In the Catholic tradition, such legitimate power was often vested to a great degree in priests and nuns. To Catholics who attended parochial schools in the first half of the twentieth century, few phrases were as powerful as "Sister said...." If a person did not accept the influence or compulsion that the legitimate power source was attempting to effect, all the forces inside the system would impose a certain guilt on that person. Rejecting the influence of the legitimate power source would be tantamount to rejecting the values inherent in the system.

*Raven and French use "P" and "O" to designate the two people in the power relationship. I suspect that many people, including myself, feel as though they are reading algebra when they see a few pages of type with symbols strewn over them. To avoid that effect, I use two common names in the explanations: "Frances," for the one who holds the power; and "John," for the one over whom the power is exercised.

The fourth category is *referent power.* John allows Frances to influence his conduct because of a desire for a close relationship with her. Identification is therefore the basis for this power.[34] John is perhaps attracted to Frances or has other reasons for wanting to be close to her, so he says, "I will become more intimately related to Frances if I do what Frances tells me to do." Consequently, Frances gains significant control over John.

The final category is *expert power.*[35] If John perceives Frances as having great competence and superior knowledge in a certain area, he will be very open to accepting the influence or compulsion that Frances exerts on him. Being in the position of "the expert" gives Frances real authority over John and allows her to exercise power over him to the extent or degree that he perceives her expertise to be authentic.

From the written sources on collective bargaining and striking and from my interviews with union and management personnel, descriptions of experience emerged that seemed to fit well into three of these categories proposed by Raven and French. By viewing the power conflicts of human service workers and management personnel in the light of these categories, we may gain a clearer understanding of the dynamic that leads to the moment of a strike.

Chief executive officers (CEOs), middle management personnel, and sponsors of not-for-profit, voluntary, charitable, and religious institutions seem to speak and write about themselves in terms of having *legitimate power.* They own or operate their institutions solely for the benefit of their clients. They seek no profit. They usually enter into the enterprise of providing human services with the finest intentions. This rationale "legitimates" their power.

Consequently, management personnel can easily feel (I use the word "feel" here purposely rather than "think," because the experience I will describe seems to be intuitive and unconscious) that workers who question their judgments or challenge their decisions are negating the values on which the enterprise is based. To put this conflict in extreme terms for the sake of making the point, management personnel who undertake a human service enterprise solely for love of God and neighbor could feel that they have power over their institutions by "divine right." Since their motivation for acting is so altruistic, how could their employees ever question the way that the service is delivered or the conditions of and compensation for their work? To challenge the legitimate power of management personnel who are so well motivated could be interpreted as challenging the God-like reasons for which the enterprise has been founded.

On the other hand, professional human service workers look for and wish to affirm *expert power* in management. Being professionals, the workers feel free to challenge what they see as inefficient uses of power in the delivery system and thoughtless uses of power regarding their working conditions and compensation. They are not necessarily rejecting the values on which the system is built; their affirmation of the same values usually has led them into their work at the institution. Rather, they are questioning the "expertness" of management's use of power.

Human service workers perceive some expert power within themselves and wish to discover the same in management. They feel free, therefore, to challenge the traditional legitimate power which management wields. The result? Sometimes the workers think that their only option is to use *coercive power,* and so they strike. They will disrupt the system until their perceptions of a sound use of power, either with regard to the delivery system or their working conditions and compensation, have been met.

For the moment I am attempting only to *describe* the power conflict, not make any ethical comment on it. I discuss the ethical evaluation in the final part of this chapter.

Categories of power according to use

Rollo May divides power into five different experiences, according to its *use* rather than its *source.* According to this categorization, one could have power from any of the five bases just mentioned but might use the power (legitimate, expert, etc.) in five different ways.

The first use of power is *exploitative.* The person in power uses control over the subject totally for self-service. Exploitative power aims at complete control of the other person for one's own ends, whether good or bad. Slavery is the classic example; it can be benign or cruel, but it always means total possession of another human being.[36]

Manipulative power is similar to exploitative, except that it substitutes cleverness and subtlety for blunt compulsion. In May's words, it is the "superseding of the gunman by the 'con' man."[37] The power user tries to put the subject in a position where the subject can never say "no" and can never avoid the impact of the power action.

The third form of power usage is a *competitive* usage. In this case, the goal is not simply to accomplish some objective; it is to end up ahead of someone else. In its negative form, May states, it consists of one person going up *because* another person goes down.[38] An accurate image for describing this kind of power usage follows: "Only a certain amount of product is to be gained by a use of power. The more you get, the less I get. So I must prevent you from getting any, and I must get all that I can." A power struggle always involves a battle with a winner and a loser.

A *nutrient* use of power is essentially "power for the other."[39] Here the power user exerts self in order to bring about the development of other people or the community. The power user seeks to discover what is necessary for the fulfillment of others and gets personal fulfillment out of using the power to achieve it. Parents' care for their children is the most common example of this use of power.

The fifth use of power is *integrative*. The power user exerts force on others so that others will have to respond in a direct, powerful way themselves. Both parties thus exercise power and grow in power, without sacrificing their individual strength in the process. May gives an excellent example of this process from his personal experience:

> A European friend of mine, when he was in this country working on his influential ideas and forming them into a book, would offer them for criticism; but the rest of us, rightly understanding how tender ideas can be when they are being born, would politely hold back any negative reaction. But our friend would regularly react with impatience, protesting: 'I *want* you to criticize me'. By this he meant that if we proposed an *antithesis* against his *thesis*, he would be forced to reform his thinking into a new and better *synthesis*.[40]

An integrative use of power invites others into the power action, with an optimism that both will grow in the experience and neither will lose independence. This scenario can succeed well sometimes but at other times can lead to seemingly irresolvable conflicts. When applying an integrative use of power to collective bargaining in the human service areas, naturally some impasse situations will result. Modern theorists have proposed several methods for dealing with such seemingly irresolvable conflicts. These methods are discussed in detail in Chapter Seven.

May's descriptions of the different uses of power lead to some interesting interpretations of the power conflict between human service workers and management. Capitalist ventures breed a spirit of competition; a capitalist system rewards those who survive best in the midst of intense competition. As noted already in Chapters Two and Three, industrial unions became an integral part of the capitalist system. As early as the last decade of the nineteenth century, the great union pioneer, Samuel Gompers, affirmed that trade unionism presumed a capitalist system and accepted its values.[41]

Consequently, when human service unions were first formed, the only example that they had to follow was the competitive industrial union model. From the literature on service unions and from my interviews, it seems that the new unions absorbed much of the capitalist spirit of competitiveness. Consciously or unconsciously, they brought this kind of power usage to bear on the relationship between management and workers in the human service enterprises.

Union leaders' constant insistence that "no difference" exists between industrial strikes and human service strikes seems to confirm this assertion. Union leaders were thereby asserting that their relationships with CEOs, sponsoring religious communities, etc., were essentially the same as with the "barons of industry." A paper by union official Jack Barbash, "Union Philosophy and the Professional," (see Chapter Three) reflects the same presupposition.[42]

The problem that a competitive approach by a union causes in not-for-profit human service enterprises should be obvious. The sponsors of human service institutions did not enter into their enterprises primarily to seek profit, but rather to fulfill needs and to provide services that would help individuals and the human community to develop to their full humanness. Most professional workers joined in the enterprise for the same reasons. Thus, an "integrative" approach by unions might have been much more successful in bringing about a cooperative spirit from management than the competitive approach borrowed from capitalist enterprises.

Management in human service institutions has traditionally had a "nutrient" approach to clients. Management personnel have not always had a similar approach to their workers; however, if they did, they often became paternalistic or maternalistic in the process. Management often neglected an integrative approach in favor of a nutrient paternalism or maternalism.

The result of the less-than-ideal power uses was power conflict, resulting sometimes in those pejorative forms of power, exploitative and manipulative, on both sides. Perhaps it is significant that the recent AFL-CIO self-study, *The Changing Situation of Workers and Their Unions*, recommends that the union movement consider fresh approaches to labor-management relations that do not presume that an adversary relationship is an inevitable—and desirable—approach of workers to management.[43]

Power sharing

The previous discussions about the nature and uses of power lead to the same conclusion: some sharing of power is necessary if the human community and the individuals within it are to develop to their full potential. Power sharing among employers and employees becomes even more necessary when both parties have some expertise about the task being performed and both are interested in developing a service system that will enhance the human community.

The churches in the United States have specifically recognized this need for power sharing among workers and employers in their affirmations of workers' natural right to organize into unions and to bargain collectively with their employers. In his encyclical, *On Human Work* ("Laborem Exercens"), Pope John Paul II defends the right of workers to empower themselves by forming unions "for the purpose of defending (their) vital interests."[44] The pope states clearly that the power that they should seek is not a power "against others," but the "power to build a community."[45]

The encyclical states unequivocally that the workers' power must include the right to strike. Pope John Paul carefully adds that this right is conditioned by the community's essential needs.

"Essential community services... must in every case be ensured"[46] in order that strikes do not harm the innocent by paralyzing the community's socioeconomic life.

The first draft of the Catholic Bishops' "Pastoral Letter on Catholic Social Teaching and the U.S. Economy" makes the same point about power sharing through unionization and the ability to strike. The letter points out how employers frequently have greater power than employees in negotiating the conditions of employment. To achieve a balance of power, "the Church fully supports the right of workers to form unions or other associations to secure their rights to fair wages and working conditions... Unions may also legitimately resort to strikes in situations where they are the only available means for pursuing the justice owed to workers."[47]

The National Council of Churches in the United States has often added its voice of approval to the power sharing that occurs through the unionization of human service workers. The National Council affirms that the right to strike is necessary for the freedom that ensures the dignity of workers in labor-management relations. In a Labor Day message in 1967, the Council specifically included government and public employees when speaking of the right to strike: "Public employees should not be denied the right to strike solely by virtue of their public employment...." Only in "rare cases when genuine damage to the general welfare clearly outweighs the values of freedom in labor-management relations" should the right to strike be denied.[48]

Why is power sharing such a basic necessity in the human condition? *Why* is it such a basic Christian teaching? One could begin to answer these questions with the example of Jesus. As already pointed out, Jesus' primary concern with power was to "empower the powerless." He did not wish to create a situation in which they would be constantly dependent on him for their strength. He wanted them to feel their own strength and be liberated, even from dependence on him.

Rahner begins a philosophical explanation of the rationale for Christ's teaching when he states: "It [power] should be the agent of its own elimination,"[49] i.e., those in power should be working toward the freedom of those presently subject to them. The Christian teaching of universal love is manifested by an effort to make everyone free and independent.

To create a community of love, everyone in the community must have some power and freedom to make his or her decisions about what is important and must have the capacity to carry out these judgments. Love is perfect only when freedom and the power to act freely have been perfected. Of its very nature, therefore, "Christian love requires a sharing of power."[50] Thus, if they are truly loving, parents will want children to grow up and make their own decisions, teachers will want students to graduate and make their own imprint on the world, physicians and nurses will want patients to get well, etc.

To be "caught in a relationship of...inequality in strength is to be caught in a relationship of domination and submission...no matter how well-meaning the dominant partner may be."[51] No one interested in the development of the human community wants unequal relationships to endure without end. To maintain that "I want to keep domination over a group of workers in order to help other powerless people" is self-defeating. It is a contradiction of Christian love.

We have traditionally called such behavior "paternalism" or "maternalism" and have used the terms with pejorative connotations. They have come to mean that the power users attempt to keep those subject to them in the role of children permanently, to keep them powerless so that they will do what they are told and cause no problems. A refusal to share power usually means that the power holder sees the purpose of power as "getting things done" to the exclusion of "helping people to grow."

Former American Federation of State, County and Municipal Employees (AFSCME) president, Jerry Wurf, considered a power sharing that leads to the dignity of the workers as the primary issue in collective bargaining involving public service employees. Without some involvement in the machinery that controls their destiny, workers will always have to "go to the boss as a beggar," not as an equal. The final goal of power sharing is not to be able to set wages or working conditions arbitrarily; it is to raise workers to their full humanness. "The most important dynamic in our organization is the conferring of dignity on workers....The be all and end all is dignity."[52]

If power sharing is clearly a Christian teaching and a logical conclusion from a philosophy of the nature of human beings, then why is there such resistance to it in practice? At least three practical responses have been suggested in the interviews that I conducted and in the literature of labor relations and social psychology.

The first response comes from management's view of its power, especially in not-for-profit delivery systems. As noted in the discussion of the different kinds of power, management personnel often see themselves as having "legitimate" power that belongs to them by right because of their altruistic intentions. Any sharing of that power could be seen as a "gift" to the less powerful that the power holder could withdraw at any time. Thus management might easily balk at power sharing if the subjects maintain that such power is their right and not a gratuitous offering from management.[53]

A second practical reason for management in not-for-profit institutions resisting power sharing may stem from the way that such institutions set up their boards of directors or trustees. Just as the union movement has absorbed some of the spirit and trappings of the capitalist system, so have management personnel through their boards. Boards of trustees are often made up of successful business people who have worked hard in the capitalist system. Many, if not most, serve on boards of hospitals, private schools, etc., with the best intentions; however, they often bring the competitive spirit of capitalism with them.

To share power voluntarily (unless one forsees that such a sharing will bring obvious empirical advantages) is not the spirit of capitalism. To share power for reasons of shaping a more loving community and promoting individual dignity and self-worth has not been part of the American industrial spirit. Boards of trustees will often resist power sharing, even with the most well-educated and well-motivated professional service workers, because it is not the process that "has worked" in capitalist ventures.

Liberation theology has made us aware that imperfection and injustice often exist, not simply in individuals, but in the structures that imperfect human beings have fashioned. Thus, if charitable institutions uncritically accept some of those structures, they may be participating in the imperfection and even the injustice that inevitably is contained therein.

Finally, management personnel in government have resisted power sharing with employee organizations because of a philosophical adherence to the "sovereignty" theory. This argument is based on certain presuppositions about the power of public officials, especially elected officials. Such power holders have received their authority from the people democratically through free election. They represent the will of the people. Therefore, to challenge their authority is to challenge the people's will. Exponents of the sovereignty argument concerning public service strikes conclude simply and absolutely: "A public employee organization cannot argue that it more fundamentally represents the people's interest than does a duly elected representative, democratic government, and that therefore it can strike that government"[54]

The logic of the sovereignty argument does not only forbid striking; in its strict interpretation, it forbids even the sharing of power with employee organizations. Elected representatives of the people are not free to "give away" the power that the people have assigned to them. Only through the people's consent could they render this power to another agent, e.g., an employees' union.

Such a rigid interpretation of the "sovereignty" of a freely elected government in relation to employees' unions leads to untenable, absolutist positions about government's role that do not reflect the practice of U.S. government, whether federal, state, or local. Carried to its logical conclusion, the sovereignty argument could demand that the decisions of public officials should not be questioned, that public officials could not make compromises when using their power, etc.

The sovereignty argument logically concludes that employees' unions must never be permitted to usurp the power of elected representatives. To demand that unions not share in that power at all, however, is another matter. Such an interpretation of sovereignty suggests that elected officials are never free to share their power, never free to compromise, never free to invite others to help them make their decisions.

If power sharing is sound human theory as well as traditional Christian teaching, one final observation must be made before proceeding to discuss it in terms of the morality of human service strikes. Who are the powerless in our society? Who needs to benefit from power sharing the most?

Unquestionably, human service workers have suffered from the "frustration of powerlessness" to a great degree in our competitive capitalist society. A majority of the public *most in need* of these workers' services, however, have traditionally been even more powerless: the poor; minorities; children; women, especially in female-headed households; the elderly; and the disabled.[55] Although everyone receives some services from public and not-for-profit delivery systems, these six groups suffer the most if the services are not provided. Consequently, withholding human services in a strike can sometimes result in the tragic tension of the powerless being pitted against the powerless. This observation is not a judgment against service strikes, but simply a statement of a difficult reality that must be taken into account when evaluating the morality of service strikes.

Specific application of power sharing to service strikes

Three specific principles for determining the morality of service strikes may be drawn from the discussions on the nature of power and power sharing.

Principle 3

Human service strikes are morally justified when they are the only means left to the workers to obtain a proper sharing of power for developing the quality of the delivery system (as long as no disproportionate harm is done to powerless clients or to the delivery system).

Morally sound decisions are those that lead to the full development of human beings and the communities and systems of which they are a part. Since human service workers, especially professionals, have expertise to offer for shaping and improving the delivery systems in which they work, it would be immoral to thwart that expertise and not allow clients to benefit from it. For the good of any delivery system, human service workers need some sharing in power in order to help the system to be as effective as possible in aiding its clients.

This principle states that human service workers should be seeking a "proper" sharing of power. It is not proper for workers to presume to collect the expertise of everyone involved in the system, organize it, and present a final conclusion about how the system should work. Such a process is, by definition, the task of management. Service workers have a right to have their expertise, experience, and suggestions become a serious part of policy in any system. If management simply ignores or rejects their contributions, the system would weaken and clients would receive less than what should be available to them.

If the sponsors or management personnel of human service delivery systems refuse to share power with their workers and workers have used all reasonable means to persuade management to do so, then a strike could be justified (as long as no disporportionate harm is done to powerless clients or to the delivery system itself; see Chapter Six). Other ways to gain a sharing in power must have been tried first: attempts at meetings, formulation of proposals, etc. The nature of human service work requires an attempt to use integrative power before coercive power. Management and workers are presumed to have similar goals and to have entered into the enterprise for similar reasons. An integrative use of power fits their relationship much more than the competitive or coercive power that flows naturally from profit-making capitalist enterprises.

Many nurses' strikes in the last two decades have resulted apparently because of management's unwillingness to recognize that nurses should have a voice in shaping the health care delivery system. Perhaps nurses feel patronized more than most other professional human service workers because not only management, but physicians as well, seem to have a low level of appreciation for nurses' contribution to health care. A recent study of nurses' strikes reveals that nurses perceive that "administrators ignore the frustrations of the nurse, while physicians persist in regarding them not as valued health care coprofessionals, but rather as handmaidens."[56] Being subject to a patronizing attitude from two sets of professionals may indeed cause a double "frustration of powerlessness" in nurses.

Elementary and secondary school teachers are sometimes in a similar position, but apparently much more with school boards than with principals. School boards often seem to appeal, implicitly or explicitly, to the "sovereignty" argument in conflicts with teachers, i.e., that they have been empowered by the public to run the school system and that they must not share that power and responsibility with anyone. Often they use this same argument to reject compulsory binding arbitration. They will not give to a third party the right to decide on issues that belong to them through public trust.

Principle 4

Human service strikes are morally justified when they are the only means left to the workers to obtain a proper sharing in the power to determine the conditions of and compensation for their work (as long as no disproportionate harm is done to powerless clients or to the delivery system).

This principle asserts that workers must have the capacity to carry out authentic self-love. It is unhealthful in any system or community to have workers depend totally on the magnanimity of their bosses for the conditions and compensation of their work. In the interests of the full human development of everyone involved, workers must have some voice in these two issues.

From the perspective of justice, salary and decent working conditions are not free will offerings from a benign patron. Workers have a *right* to both. They also have a right to demand both, especially when serious deficiencies obviously exist in present conditions and compensation.

The total system benefits when human service workers have compensation and working conditions that allow them to live with dignity in their society. In the past, the delivery systems themselves have suffered because many people in our competitive, success-oriented society tended to look down on teachers, nurses, police, social workers, etc., because they were paid so poorly. Society's judgment reflected the idea: "People who are willing to work for such meager compensation couldn't really be very talented. They probably couldn't get good jobs in competitive industry." With such a mentality, society would respect human service workers only in a patronizing way. The same could be said about the delivery systems. They were considered valuable but not on a par with the "real world" of business and high finance.

For the sake of their own dignity and to pursue authentic self-love, human service workers could ethically strike to seek just wage and working conditions if striking were the only means left to accomplish their goals. As emphasized, all other reasonable means to obtain a just solution must have been tried first. The workers must always be sensitive to their responsibility of risking no serious or irreparable harm to their clients or to the delivery system.

Strikes that deal primarily with shaping the delivery system (Principle 3) may seem easier to justify than strikes that deal with the workers' compensation and working conditions (Principle 4). From the perspective of contemporary ethics and moral theology, such is *not* the case; it only *seems so* because of the traditional bias that our Western tradition has had against self-love and assertiveness. As we noted in Principle 2, the workers' ordinary needs and the client's ordinary needs are comparable realities and should be considered to have equal value. A strike about wages (when a clear injustice exists) could be as well justified as a strike about the quality of service being given to clients (when it is clearly deficient).

Principle 5

For power seeking in human service strikes to be morally justified, workers must be ultimately seeking *integrative* rather than *competitive* power.

An action is "moral" when it helps to bring individuals or communities to their full human development. Immoral actions tend to disrupt development and prevent people and communities or systems from reaching their full potential.

In human services, competitive power most often tends to be disruptive. Competition naturally results in a "winner" and a "loser." Competition always involves some desire to "get ahead" of the other person and to gain power that will put one in a more advantageous position than the other. Competition always connotes an adversary position. One person's victory comes through the other's defeat.

In human services, since management and workers presumably are involved in the enterprise for many of the same reasons, having winners and losers almost always damages the system.[57] Management and workers compete *against* one another instead of using all their energies *for* the goals of the human service enterprise. To stand in a constant adversarial relationship drains energy and is not conducive to the kind of cooperation that creates the most productive human service delivery system.

Integrative power fits the relationship between human service workers and management more accurately. This use of power tends to bring out the strengths of both parties without having winners and losers. The description of integrative power presented earlier and that of assertive loving behavior are remarkably similar. In both cases, people act from a source of strength within themselves in order to face reality as it is, with the hope that the people with whom they are interacting will do the same.

Human service workers challenge management personnel to raise their awareness concerning justice to the workers and better ways of delivering services to the clients. Management challenges workers to evoke the best use of their talents and make them aware of both the possibilities and the limitations of the systems in which they are involved.

If the descriptions of the Atlanta firefighters' strike (1966) in the newspapers and journals were accurate, it would be a classic example of a human service strike aimed at competitive rather than integrative power. According to the accounts, the actual reason for the strike was a union jurisdictional dispute. One union wanted to "break" another union and thus gain power.[58] The city suffered some serious harm through numerous false alarms, two fires started by Molotov cocktails, and an atmosphere of unrest, especially downtown. The relationships between union members were also greatly damaged as they opted for the two opposing unions. The real emphasis was not on the workers' development (compensation and working conditions) or on the delivery system's development (more professional ways of firefighting), but on a power victory over a competing union.

An interview with teachers who had gone through a creative approach to collective bargaining ("collective gaining," which I discuss in the Chapter Seven), gives another example of how the competitive power approach can be disruptive. The teachers' union and management had agreed to bargain through this very nonadversarial method to streamline the bargaining process and to eliminate all posturing and time-consuming tactics. The process worked. The previous bargaining period had been about a year. With the new process, the parties came to an agreement in a few months. The union received almost exactly what it had hoped to gain in salary and benefit increases.

One small faction within the union, however, strongly opposed the union leaders who made the settlement. Their attitude was: "If you could get that much from management in such a short time, then you should never have settled. You should have continued—even to the point of striking—until you got a lot more!" They did not take issue with the conditions of the settlement giving them a decent compensation (according to *their own* preset standards), and reasonable working conditions and allowing the system to continue to deliver its service without tension. Their point was that the union might have obtained *more* if it had used more competitive, or coercive, power. In such a case, "getting more" becomes a greater value than all the other values. This attitude inevitably will damage the community and the system through tensions, poor relationships, and value conflicts.

The pursuit of competitive power in human service systems can often be destructive or at least drain energy away from the main goal of delivering valuable human services to clients in need. The pursuit of integrative power most often is fulfilling to both management and workers; consequently, it allows clients to be touched by a system whose energies are directly focused on the human development of everyone involved.

Notes

1. Thomas McMahon, "The Moral Aspects of Power," in Franz Boeckle and Jacques-Marie Pohier, eds., *Power and the Word of God* (Concilium, vol. 90) (New York: Herder & Herder, 1983), p. 60.

2. Rollo May, *Power and Innocence* (New York: W.W. Norton & Co., 1972), p. 114.

3. Romano Guardini, *Power and Responsibility* (Chicago: H. Regnery Co., 1961), p. 14.

4. May, p. 25.

5. Edgar Z. Friedenberg, *Coming of Age in America* (New York: Random House, 1965), pp. 47-48.

6. Karl Rahner, "The Theology of Power," in *Theological Investigations*, vol. IV (New York: Crossroad Publications, 1982), p. 400.

7. McMahon, p. 57.

8. Rahner, p. 399.

9. Elizabeth Janeway, *Powers of the Weak* (New York: Alfred A. Knopf, 1980), p. 88.

10. Jacob Burckhardt, *Force and Freedom: Reflections on History*, James Hastings Nichols, ed., (New York: Pantheon Books, 1943), p. 184.

11. *Quotations from Chairman Mao Tse-Tung* (Peking: Foreign Languages Press, 1966), p. 61.

12. James Hanigan, "Spiritual Life and the Uses of Power," *Studies in Formative Spirituality* V:3 (November 1984), p. 344.

13. Hanigan, pp. 336-337.

14. Hanigan, pp. 342-344.

15. May, p. 113.

16. Guardini, p. 2.

17. Rahner, p. 391.

18. Max Weber, *Economy and Society*, Guenther Roth and Claus Wittich, eds., (New York: Bedminster Press, 1968), vol. 1, sec. 16, p. 53.

19. Hannah Arendt, *On Violence* (New York: Harcourt, Brace and World, Inc., 1969), p. 25.

20. Paul Tillich, *Love, Power, and Justice* (New York: Oxford University Press, 1960), p. 47.

21. For other interesting collections of power definitions from philosophers and social psychologists, see Samuel B. Bacharach and Edward J. Lawler, *Power and Politics in Organizations* (San Francisco: Jossey-Bass Publishers, 1980), pp. 16-17; and Dorwin Cartwright, "A Field Theoretical Conception of Power," in *Studies in Social Power* (University of Michigan, Ann Arbor: Research Center for Group Dynamics, Institute for Social Research, 1959), pp. 186-187. These definitions give different perspectives on the phenomenon but essentially contain the five characteristics distilled from the definitions in the text.

22. Tillich, p. 67.

23. Jean Guichard, "Ideologies and Power," in Franz Boeckle and Jacques-Marie Pohier, eds., *Power and the Word of God* (Concilium, vol. 90) (New York: Herder & Herder, 1973), p. 90.

24. Janeway, p. 89.

25. Martin Hengel, *Christ and Power* (Philadelphia: Fortress Press, 1977), pp. 15-17.

26. For a fine, brief analysis of Jesus' critique of the powerful, see Gustavo Gutierrez, *A Theology of Liberation* (Maryknoll, NY: Orbis Books, 1973), pp. 297-302.

27. Yves Congar, *Power and Poverty in the Church* (Baltimore: Helicon Press, 1964), pp. 21-39.

28. Hengel, pp. 16-17.

29. James Reese, "The Event of Jesus—Power in Flesh," in Franz Boeckle and Jacques-Marie Pohier, eds., *Power and the Word of God* (Concilium, vol. 90) (New York: Herder & Herder, 1973), p. 48.

30. John R.P. French, Jr., and Bertram Raven, "The Bases of Social Power," in Darwin Cartwright, ed., *Studies in Social Power* (University of Michigan, Ann Arbor: Research Center for Group Dynamics, Institute for Social Research, 1959), pp. 150-167.

31. French and Raven, p. 156.

32. French and Raven, p. 157.

33. French and Raven, p. 159. Elementary school teachers generally had great legitimate power in U.S. communities in that period. English police ("bobbies") had an almost legendary legitimate power until a few decades ago when they began to carry handguns.

34. French and Raven, pp. 161-162.

35. French and Raven, pp. 163-164. Raven and A.W. Kruglanski added a sixth category in 1970, which is really a subdivision of "expert power." They call it "information power." It differs from "expert power" in that it exists in a single encounter or dialogue where one person has the information that another person needs in order to function. With expert power, the expert continually remains in the power position. See B.H. Raven and A.W. Kruglanski, "Conflict and Power," in P. Swingle, ed., *The Structure of Conflict* (New York: Academic Press, 1970).

36. May, pp. 105-106.

37. May, p. 106.

38. May, pp. 107-108.

39. May, p. 109.

40. May, p. 109.

41. Daniel Bell, "Industrial Conflict and Public Opinion," and Frederick H. Harbison, "Collective Bargaining and American Capitalism," in A. Kornhauser, R. Dubin, and A. Ross, eds., *Industrial Conflict* (New York: McGraw-Hill, 1954), pp. 243, 278.

42. Jack Barbash, "Union Philosophy and the Professional" (unpublished paper for Department of Labor Studies, Pennsylvania State University, 1978). Barbash insists that in employer-employee relationships, "the character of the work makes little difference" concerning the way that the parties will deal with problems, that neither side can ever be trusted "to protect adequately the interests of the other," and that even in education and other service enterprises "the employer wants to get more money out of the business and keep costs down...the employee wants to earn or save more money...." Barbash implies that an adversary relationship, based on competitive power, is inevitable for all employers and employees.

43. AFL-CIO Committee on the Evolution of Work, *The Changing Situation of Workers and Their Unions* (Washington, DC: AFL-CIO Publication No. 165, 1985), pp. 18-19.

44. John Paul II, "Laborem Exercens," English translation in *Origins* 11:15 (Sept. 24, 1981), p. 239.

45. John Paul II, p. 239.

46. John Paul II, p. 240.

47. National Conference of Catholic Bishops, *Pastoral Letter on Catholic Social Teaching and the U.S. Economy* (first draft) (Washington, DC: United States Catholic Conference, 1984), pp. 37-38.

48. "Major Faiths Sound Themes of Racial Justice, Right To Strike," in R.E. Walsh, ed., *Sorry...No Government Today* (Boston: Beacon Press, 1969), p. 232.

49. Rahner, p. 406.

50. McMahon, p. 56.

51. Hanigan, pp. 340-341.

52. See an interview with Jerry Wurf in Richard N. Billings and John Greenya, *Power to the Public Worker* (Washington, DC and New York: Robert B. Luce, Inc., 1974), pp. 208-210, 218.

53. Janeway, p. 85.

54. Sar A. Levitan and Alexandra B. Noden, *Working for the Sovereign: Employee Relations in the Federal Government* (Baltimore: Johns Hopkins University Press, 1983), p. 6.

55. Richard A. McCormick, *Health and Medicine in the Catholic Tradition* (New York: Crossroad Publishing Co., 1984), p. 75.

56. Norman Metzger, Joseph M. Ferentino, and Kenneth F. Kruger, *When Health Care Employees Strike* (Rockville, MD: Aspen Systems Corp., 1984), p. 91.

57. Note here that I am not making any absolutist judgments about competition itself. In certain areas of human endeavor, competition may indeed be helpful and the cause of growth. Some modern psychologists, however, question the value of competition in many, if not most, genuinely human enterprises. (See Henri J. M. Nouwen, *Creative Ministry* [New York: Image Books, 1978], pp. 5-8.) I am speaking only of its place in not-for-profit, directly delivered, necessary human service systems.

58. "What Does a City Do When Firemen Go on Strike?" in R.E. Walsh, ed., *Sorry...No Government Today* (Boston: Beacon Press, 1969), pp. 54-58.

Chapter 6

Rights of Clients
and the "Harm" Issue

No one should hurt anyone else.

What could be more basic to a sound morality? Good human beings do not inflict harm on others and do not destroy what is fulfilling in others' lives.

Life, however, is complex. Even when human beings are doing what seem to be eminently good actions, someone somewhere may be hurt. A person speaks a word in behalf of justice for minorities in the United States, and someone in power is offended. Another person goes out of her way to help a neighbor, and a second neighbor feels slighted. So many intricate ramifications are involved in even our ordinary actions that it is impossible to avoid harming others at least on some occasions.

In a sound ethic, we begin with a realization that human life is imperfect, that our relationships are so complex that some harm may be done even when we are acting our best. In a sound ethic we strive to avoid purposely causing any harm to others. We also seek to bring about more good effects than bad when our actions may inevitably cause some harm.

In human service strikes, the primary concern of almost everyone involved has been to avoid causing direct harm to the clients, who are often caught helplessly in the middle of a conflict between management and workers. Most people agree that to intend to cause direct harm to the clients is almost always immoral (exceptions could exist in some extreme cases) and should painstakingly be avoided. Before formulating principles about the role of harm in the shaping of ethical judgments about human service strikes, however, we must first articulate clearly what "harm" is.

The nature of harm

In keeping with the approach to morality that we have taken in this book, "harm" is defined here in terms of damage to, or the prevention of, the human development of persons and communities or systems. To harm some persons, communities, or systems is to prevent them from reaching their full development, or to destroy some of the development already achieved.

Thus punishing criminals by imprisonment or disciplining children by forbidding them to engage in a favorite entertainment is not "harm" in this technical sense. Such actions should benefit the persons involved. These actions cause difficulties and even pain for those subjected to them, but they are not "harmful" in that they do not impede development. The actions may even promote their development. Not all pain, trial, and inconvenience are harmful.

True harm can be understood both as physical damage and as relational damage. To suffer a broken bone in a robbery, to have a minor illness become serious because it went untreated, or to suffer burns in a fire are forms of physical harm. To have a friendship or a working relationship disrupted, to lose confidence in a professional who was helping to maintain the stability of one's life, or to lose an educational opportunity are all forms of relational damage. Each takes something away, physically or relationally, from the growth and development of a person or a community.

One further clarification must be made about the kind of harm that we are discussing in relation to human service strikes. It is a harm that is always passive in nature, i.e., it is "allowed to happen," and is not directly inflicted on a client. Teachers, nurses, police, firefighters, and social workers do not directly inflict any damage on their clients when they strike. They *withhold* their services. Possible harm may come from their actions, but it is not directly willed or positively inflicted on clients. Thus we are concerned about harm that *may* happen, that could *possibly* occur.

I am not thereby absolving human service workers from responsibility for such harm. I am only stating that the causal connection between withdrawing their services and consequent harm is more tenuous and uncertain than harm caused by physical attacks on persons or verbal attacks on their character. In these cases, the causal connection is direct and immediate. In speaking of harm caused by service strikes, we must always be careful to point out that the harm is potential, it could possibly occur, but that it is not certain and immediate. There is a risk of harm in a human service strike, but not certain harm to the clients or to the system.

Two kinds of harm

From an analysis of the effects of human service strikes, as described in the literature I reviewed and the interviews I conducted, I suggest that the resulting harm can be categorized under two headings: *irreparable*, or *serious*, harm; and *inconveniencing* harm.

I use the term "irreparable harm" because it has already become a standard term in the laws of many states and is frequently used in court decisions for enjoining human service strikes. The term must not be taken literally, however, since one could argue theoretically that almost any harm done in the human condition could be repaired if one had the time and energy and resources to do so. Also—and this is a point that the courts seem to have missed—human service strikes cause some forms of harm that are reparable but are nonetheless destructive to human values and very different from temporary inconveniences. Thus, in trying to determine the morality of human service strikes, I use the adjectives "irreparable" and "serious" to describe experiences of harm that are equally important. These terms are used according to the following definitions.

The term "irreparable" must be understood in a reasonable way that fits the experience of most people. As noted, almost any harm could be repaired if one had unlimited resources at one's disposal, i.e., access to a host of the most skilled professional people in the world, adequate funds, and the most refined technical equipment. It would be foolish to use the term 'irreparable" in this sense, since such conditions are almost never realized.

In this discussion, irreparable refers to harm that is *ordinarily not repaired* according to the conditions in which most people find themselves in our culture. Harm could be called irreparable if a person lost an educational opportunity that probably would not present itself again; if a person suffered a permanent physical disability because of lack of immediate emergency room treatment; or if a client became so depressed because the counseling process was suddenly interrupted that he or she just could not find the energy to begin again. Irreparable is used to connote the harm that most people do not have the time and energy and resources to repair in the ordinary life-style of our culture.

The highly theoretical definition of the term, however, often used by the courts when they are pursuing the sovereignty argument (see Chapter Five), is not included here, since such use does not seem to fit anyone's real experience. In the *Buffalo Board of Education v. Pisa* decision, the court proclaims: "By its very nature a strike by public employees constitutes an 'irreparable injury' to the public order and welfare."[1]

New York Supreme Court Justice Samuel M. Gold makes the same highly theoretical point when he writes that in public service strikes "the greatest and most irreparable damage by far is the defiance of government authority as duly established by law."[2] As already argued, such statements simply do not seem to fit the facts. Our governing bodies do not appear to be permanently damaged by such strikes, our legal system does not seem to be permanently disordered, and the authority of elected officials does not seem to be significantly weakened.

Some forms of harm caused by human service strikes may be very serious but reparable. During a police strike, a citizen attacked by a criminal may return to perfect health after six months of treatment. A person who suffers serious burns in a fire during a firefighters' strike may look perfectly normal after plastic surgery and a year of recuperation. We could hardly call such incidents temporary inconvenience and place them in the same category with delaying elective surgery. Even though the harm was reparable, it caused a serious disruption of human life and development. Such harm should be put on the same level as irreparable harm, because it causes a large gap in a person's human growth and development, is traumatic to deal with, and very difficult to overcome.

On the other hand, temporary inconveniences, delays, and occasional obstacles to human growth are part of human development. To experience such inconveniences and obstacles because of a service strike is nothing extraordinary. These inconveniences do slow down our progress to full humanness, but they do not take it away or seriously impair it.

Such inconveniences, delays, and obstacles do fit our technical definition of harm: they damage or prevent full human development. The damage can always be repaired, however, and the loss always recouped. Temporary inconvenience and trial are part of the ordinary struggle of life, often resulting in satisfying human growth.

There is an important reason for distinguishing inconveniencing harm from irreparable and serious harm. In most human service strikes, the workers perceive themselves as suffering from similar temporary and inconveniencing obstacles to their own human development. In a strike, the inconvenience to the clients is often being weighed against the conditions that adversely affect the workers' development. As seen in our discussion of self-love, to weigh equal needs against one another can be authentic and loving Christian behavior. It is another matter for workers to weigh their needs to overcome obstacles to their own development against permanent damage to their clients. A few other examples, some based on actual incidents from human service strikes in the past two decades, should serve to make this distinction more clear.

For some people, delaying elective surgery for a month because of a nurses' strike can be annoying and disruptive to their plans. The surgery, however, if it truly fits the description of "elective," can be done later, safely, and without any permanent harm to the patient other than some lingering anger because of the inconvenience. It is different if adequate emergency services are not available during a nurses' strike and a person with a crucial need is not served and sustains a permanent disability. Similarly, if a person who is recuperating from major surgery is left without adequate nursing care, especially in an intensive care unit, the damage to that person could be most serious and even fatal.

Students may suffer some delay in their development because of a two- or three-week teachers' strike (although the studies to date indicate that no noticeable effect on their education occurs, even if the strike lasts for two months[3]), and parents may suffer some inconvenience because of having to adjust their schedules. However, the inconvenience to both is no greater than that caused by occasional illnesses and results in no lasting disruption to their lives. On the other hand, rare cases have occurred, especially in inner-city schools, in which strikes have permanently damaged minority students who were finally beginning to overcome years of deprivation and enter seriously and interestedly into the academic enterprise. A strike lasting several weeks interrupted their progress, and they never regained their interest or enthusiasm for education.

A strike by food-service personnel in nursing homes might cause some discomfort to the elderly residents and deprive them of one of the few, small joys in their life-style. Rarely, however, would such a strike cause more than some temporary complaints by the residents and inconvenience for the administrators. A strike by nurses that would cause nursing home clientele to be relocated to another facility, however, could result in permanent harm to the elderly. Many people in such institutions depend so completely on the security, routine, and familiar surroundings that a move to another location could permanently impair mental clarity and emotional stability. The quality of life in their remaining years could be irreparably damaged.

One of the most dramatic examples of this kind of damage reportedly occurred during the 47-day strike against the voluntary hospitals and nursing homes in New York in 1984. According to a prominent figure in the strike negotiations, when some eldery residents of a Jewish nursing home were being taken on a bus to another facility, they went through the same traumatic feelings they experienced when they were being transported to a concentration camp in Germany during World War II. They were so traumatized by the experience that they were never able to regain the composure, security, and clarity of mind they had before the strike, even after they were returned to the security of the nursing home.

Harm that inconveniences and harm that seriously or irreparably damages people are clearly distinct realities and clearly different human experiences. It is extremely difficult to justify causing irreparable or serious harm to innocent clients in human service strikes. On the other hand, it is often possible to justify some inconveniencing harm to clients for the sake of attaining other important goals. The final section of this chapter argues that a sound ethical position on service strikes should be based to some degree on this distinction.

An analysis of rights

A brief analysis of the rights of clients and human service workers illustrates more clearly the ethical dimensions of harm to clients during a strike. Are clients' rights harmed by a strike? The answer depends on one's position concerning the complex issue of a "*right* to health care, a *right* to education and a *right* to public safety."[4] Can we speak of these three areas in terms of strict rights?

Discussing the issue of rights clearly requires a contemporary understanding of the nature of a right. A right is not a *thing*, nor is it a service due to us. In precise language, a right is a *relationship*. When speaking about a presumed right to health care, the health care is not the right. The right is the person's relationship to that service, a relationship that is due in justice.[5] When we speak of a right to any object or any service, we mean that people *ought* to have a relationship of possession or control of the object, a relationship of reception to the service.

We may relate to anything to which we have a right in either a positive or a negative way.[6] In a positive relationship, the thing or object we have a right to should be rendered to us; we should not have to beg, fight, or work to get it. For example, once we have paid for an object in a department store, the clerks should simply give it to us, without acting as if they are doing something special for us. When we receive our paychecks at the end of the month, they should be given with no hint of patronizing generosity on the part of the employer.

By a negative relationship we mean that, although we have no claim to having another agent freely render the object or service to us, we may demand that no one interfere with our pursuit of the right. The right to life is a good example of a negative right. No other agent is bound to render a full development of life to us. Rather, all other agents are bound not to interfere as we pursue human growth and fulfillment; they are bound not to injure or destroy our life. The right to liberty or freedom is another example. This right does not obligate anyone else to make our choices for us or to fulfill them once we have made them. It simply binds others not to limit or take away our freedom, as long as we are using it justly without intruding on the rights of others.

According to most scholars, those rights we have traditionally called basic human rights or natural rights[7] are ours in a negative way. Some would list freedom, equality, and participation[8] as the foundational rights that belong to all persons simply because they are creatures of God and exist as human beings. From a more political point of view, other scholars suggest that the following six rights are basic to being human: (1) to live, (2) to enjoy and preserve a cultural identity, (3) to take part in decision making within society, (4) to hold different opinions, (5) to have personal dignity, and (6) to choose one's own religion.[9]

These basic human rights are sometimes called "general rights"[10] or "universal rights."[11] Everyone has them by virtue of being human; all other agents have a duty not to interfere with them or take them away.

The rights that belong to people in a positive way are also called special rights, claim rights, or particular rights.[12] These rights arise from a contract, either explicit or implicit, between two agents. They are conditional in that they continue to exist as long as the contract is in place and has not been justly terminated by both parties. A person has a right to six violin lessons once that person has made proper arrangements with a teacher and paid the fee. A person has a right to vote if that person has fulfilled the proper requirements for citizenship and registered before the election. While the "relationship of dueness" lasts, the one who has the right may positively demand the object or service from the other agent. Special rights are conditional, limited in scope, and grounded in particular relationships.

Right to health care, education, and public safety

Do the citizens of our society have, in an accurate technical sense, rights to health care, education, and public safety? Much contemporary ethical literature, as well as the language of law and the courts, affirms that citizens do have such rights. Richard McCormick writes that "several of the popes...the American Catholic bishops, the American Medical Association, and an accumulating bioethical literature have asserted that there is a right to health care."[13] Recent studies of education and health care in the United States come to the same conclusion.[14]

Political philosophers, however, do not agree on exactly what kind of right people have to these services.[15] It seems reasonable to speak of a general (negative) right, since these services are simply ways to carry out the obvious fundamental rights to life, liberty, the pursuit of personal happiness, and fulfillment. Thus they may be considered extensions, or more specific determinations, of these fundamental human rights. No other agent in our society, therefore, should impede any citizen in the pursuit of health care, education, and a safe, secure life in U.S. society.

Can we say more than this general affirmation that citizens have the right to pursue these services? Is it overstating the case to suggest that some agents in our society have the duty, the responsibility in strict justice, to provide these services to citizens? This issue is precisely what is disputed today by political theorists, philosophers, and theologians: whether or not the right to these services can be called a special (positive) right. For the practical purposes of this study, it is possible to give an answer to this complicated question without resolving all the difficult theoretical issues about justice and rights that undergird the dispute.

In the development of our Western society, a consensus has developed among citizens that a certain level of education, health care, and public safety is absolutely necessary for living a decent life.[16] Without it, the rights to life, liberty, etc., are meaningless. This consensus among citizens is given practical expression by the duly elected representative government of society. The government assures the citizens that they have these rights—some would even say that the government "confers" the rights[17]—and accepts the responsibility for overseeing the rendering of the services.

Whether the ensuing contract between the government and its citizens fits exactly the philosophical conditions for creating a strict right to education, health care, and public safety is debatable. In practice, the contract between the U.S. government and its citizens does mean that, if individual citizens or groups of citizens are not able to secure these services on their own, the government accepts the responsibility of either providing or securing the services for the citizens. In this practical sense, citizens do have a special (positive) right to health, education, and public safety.

Conflict of rights in a strike

Even if one accepts this practical conclusion about a right to health care, education, and public safety, there remains an uncertainty about who specifically is bound in justice to render the services. Consequently, the question of human service strikes is not resolved by pointing to this special right and stating, "Citizens have a right to these public services; therefore, workers cannot deny citizens their rights by striking."

Since special rights depend on agreements or contracts between two parties, it is reasonable to conclude that when a contract runs out, the rights and duties connected to it no longer exist. Since strikes, at least "legal" strikes, take place only when contracts run out, the human service workers involved clearly are not rejecting a positive duty, since they are not contractually responsible for rendering the service to the clients involved. In other words, even though clients have a right to the service, they do not necessarily have the right to have the service delivered by this specific group of human service workers.

When no alternative sources are available for the service, however, one could argue that clients *do* have a right to the service at a specific facility. An example of this situation is a hospital in a rural area with no other major health care facility. A strike in such a rural hospital might deprive clients of their general right to health care.

During a strike the clients still have the right to the services that have been withdrawn. They may justly exercise that right by going to other agents to have their needs fulfilled, e.g., to other physicians and nurses or to another hospital. There is no reason why they may not exercise their right by organizing a temporary service system while the regular services are not available, e.g., a neighborhood tutoring service or special classes to prepare for college board examinations. One could likewise argue that, since society has accepted the responsibility for rendering the services, society could provide other means for fulfilling the services during the strike.

This argument for accepting or providing alternative services during a strike is valid because clients have a general (negative) right to the services; no other agents in society have the right to prevent clients from seeking and accepting these human services. Therefore, the direct intention of human service workers in striking must *not* be to deprive clients of their right to human services. For a human service strike to be just from its inception, workers must intend primarily to pressure management by inconveniencing them through a temporary disruption of the delivery system.

Putting the position of the strikers and the clients in the form of a dialogue may clarify this discussion. The strikers are saying to the clients: "We are not intending to harm you or to interfere with your rights. We intend to put pressure on management to achieve our just demands, which improve the delivery system and enhance our dignity as human beings. We will not permit you to suffer any irreparable harm. We realize that you may suffer some temporary harm in the process, but that is not our intention. If some harm does occur, we will do our best to repair it in the future."

The clients respond: "We respect your right not to work and to challenge a system that you find to be unjust to you, or inefficient in delivering human services. But we need to receive some of these services now, especially the ones that we perceive to be most important to us personally. We realize that our pursuit of these services while you are on strike may take away some of the force of your strike, but our intention is not to harm the effectiveness of your action. Our intention is to pursue our own human development. If some harm is done to you or your union in the process, we will do our best to minimize it."

Unlike industrial strikes, some conflict of rights always exists in human service strikes, precisely because clients with rights are always involved. Although the workers are not bound in strict justice to render the services to the clients, they are bound not to interfere with the clients' pursuit of their rights. To enforce "nonservice" on the clients would be to intrude on the clients' general right to health care, education, and public safety.

Consequently, the question of "scab labor" and "strikebreaking" is a far more complex issue in human service strikes than in industrial strikes. A neighbor who comes to a nursing home during a strike to care for a few elderly friends is essentially fulfilling their right to basic health care. The neighbor's action may indirectly have a minor weakening effect on the pressure of the strike, but her immediate purpose is not to cause harm to the workers' strike action, just as the workers' immediate goal is not to cause harm to the clients.

How can this conflict of rights be resolved? It probably cannot be resolved perfectly, but it is my hope that an understanding of the ethical issues involved will give some direction in handling the conflict. The next section investigates the ethical principles that give some basis for evaluating the complexities of this conflict.

Specific application of harm and
rights to service strikes

Three principles for determining the morality of human service strikes may be drawn from the discussion of conflicting rights and the kinds of harm done in strikes.

Principle 6

For human service strikes to be ethical, workers must intend to exert the direct pressure of the strike on management by disrupting (causing temporary inconvenience to) the delivery system.[18]

In any strike the conflict or disagreement is with the managers and owners, not with the consumers or clients. For the confrontation to be honest and direct, the workers must intend to exert pressure on those who are responsible for the conflict and have the power to resolve the impasse.[19] It would be unethical to "use" other people to win the struggle. Consequently, in human service strikes when clients are caught in the middle of the confrontation, strikers must clearly intend not to cause harm to the clients, but to pressure management and owners by temporarily disrupting the system which management and owners control.

Service workers do not withdraw their services because they want to leave the clients unattended. Rather, they want to effect a situation in which those who control the delivery system will not be able to run the system as they wish. The pressure of the strike does not come directly from the inconvenience to the clients, but from the temporary powerlessness that owners and management experience because of it.

To deprive owners and management of their capacity to run the system as they wish does put great pressure on them. A comparison to industrial strikes may be helpful here in understanding the exact nature of this pressure. Whereas owners and managers receive profit as their primary reward in industry, owners and managers in not-for-profit human services receive (besides their salaries) such things as prestige for excellent management, a good public record, and a reputation for fairness. Intense pressure is put on not-for-profit owners and managers when they experience the public confrontation of a strike in which their management skills, their record for fairness, etc., are challenged. This pressure is especially great when "management" is a school board or another group of elected officials whose future careers depend on the skill with which they operate the delivery system and deal with such controversies.

Strikers also have a right to take measures to prevent management from simply replacing them and continuing with the delivery of the service as though the strike were not happening. Such action by management would allow them to avoid facing the issues that precipitated the strike, issues for which they have major responsibility. There is certainly something unethical about evading the problem by mass firing and replacement.[20] It would be even worse, however, for strikers to try to prevent clients from going to alternative sources for the service.

Inconvenience to the clients does not necessarily cause the primary pressure of a human service strike; the public disruption of the delivery system causes the real pressure. The strikers, therefore, must realize that they do not necessarily gain any leverage from making certain that no one else serves the clients. Just as a strike by Ford workers is not neutralized if consumers buy GM cars during the strike, so human service strikes are not neutralized if their clients go elsewhere to receive the services they need. As the next principle shows, it can be even unethical for strikers to attempt to prevent clients from seeking and receiving services elsewhere.

Some have argued that it is merely semantics to distinguish between the disruption of the system and harm to the clients. From the experience of more than two decades of human service strikes, abundant evidence shows that the distinction is real. In many nurses' strikes, the unions have made careful plans to cover all emergency services, to provide full care for patients who were already hospitalized, and to advise the public who wish elective surgery and other noncritical treatment about available services at other nearby hospitals. Often nurses' unions recommend that *all patients* be transferred to other facilities.[21]

In some police strikes, careful planning beforehand takes into account this real distinction between disrupting the system and intruding upon the rights of the clients. One police union official boasted that the union had "more people on the streets" during a midwestern police strike than the city did when service was normal. He explained that the union was trying to make the point that the police personnel, even during a strike, were more concerned about protecting the public than were the city officials who permitted the strike.

It would be naive to suggest that, even when the energies of a strike are conscientiously directed against management, no harm will be done to the clients. Clients almost always experience at least some inconvenience and temporary harm. In our discussion of Principle 8 we will consider when such harm renders a strike unethical.

Some have argued that, even when unions direct their energies against the system rather than against the clients, they still cause undue harm to one group of people, the management personnel. In some hospital strikes, supervisory personnel often work 12-hour days, seven days a week, for the duration of the strike. They undergo great physical and emotional strain as they attempt to keep the delivery system functioning. From the point of view of strict justice, causing such stress can be a fair way to carry out the confrontation. In the strikers' minds, the management personnel are equally responsible, along with the union, for the failure of the collective bargaining process to resolve their differences. Thus, the pressure should be touching precisely those people who are responsible for the conflict. Striking workers experience the stress of no income, uncertainty about the future, and anxiety about their clients. Management personnel experience the great stress of long hours of extra work, and some of the same anxieties and uncertainties as the workers. The less involved the clients, the more the strike confrontation is a "fair fight."

In summary, human service workers must intend to exert the direct pressure of a strike against management and owners, not against the clients who are caught in the middle of the conflict, powerless to do anything about it. Intense pressure can be exerted in this way, even if clients receive services from other sources. If striking workers, however, intend to pressure management *by means of* depriving clients of services and take means to prevent clients from seeking those services elsewhere, then the ethical complexion of the strike changes dramatically, as the next principle shows.

Principle 7

Human service strikes are unethical when they prevent clients from pursuing their general and special rights to health care, education, and public safety.

The preceding discussion of the rights of U.S. citizens concluded that all have a general (negative) right and, in the limited sense proposed, a special (positive) right to health care, education, and public safety. According to this *negative* right, all citizens must have the freedom to pursue adequate health care, education, and public safety without interference from any agent in society. Since the *positive* right arises from the consensus of society expressed by the state laws of the state, the government has the duty to secure these three means of human development for citizens when they are unable to attain them on their own.

According to most ethical systems, it is wrong to attempt to deprive people of their rights (except, some would argue, in the most extreme situations), no matter how noble the goal that one is seeking. Likewise, it is unethical to attempt to create situations in which people will be unable to pursue their rights.

In more concrete language, strikers have no right to attempt to prevent clients from going to alternative sources to fulfill their rights to health care, education, and public safety. Nor do strikers have the right to create a situation (e.g., a general hospital strike in a city, a general firefighters' strike in a city) in which no health care or fire protection would be available. If, in such a situation, citizens would seek to make these services available from alternative sources, strikers would have no right to prevent such sources from serving the people.

The reason for these assertions is obvious. Management, not the clients, must be the direct target for the pressure of the strike. No one has the right to risk serious harm to others to pursue personal ends (except, perhaps, in the most extreme situations), even when those ends are good in themselves. Admittedly, the clients may experience some harm amid the complexities of the strike, but the harm must not be the means whereby the strikers achieve their goals.

The following scenario expresses this principle concretely. Management and workers are engaged in an irresolvable dispute in the collective bargaining process. A strike seems inevitable, so all the clients leave the delivery system temporarily; management and workers continue their confrontation in an empty facility. Meanwhile, the clients have gone elsewhere to continue their own human growth and development. They return to the facility when management and workers have resolved their dispute.

No strike ever takes place this neatly. I use the scene only to make a basic point. No one has a right to deprive clients, especially those who are innocent and powerless, of their right to pursue their human development. Everyone should do his or her best not to involve the clients and allow the clients to continue pursuing their rights.

A dramatic example of this principle comes from a firefighters' strike in Yonkers, NY, in 1981. Volunteer firefighters from neighboring towns came at midnight to fight a fire that had broken out in an abandoned building. The fire was spreading to neighboring buildings that were occupied. Some city firefighters pushed and shoved the volunteers and prevented them from taking their hoses off the truck.[22] The volunteers retreated, and several residences were severely damaged.

It is difficult to imagine that there could ever be reasons to justify the deprivation of firefighting protection in a strike, even if crucial issues were involved. The rights not to be severely harmed by fire and to have one's residence preserved seem so immediate and apparent that no reason seems grave enough to justify taking such risks with the basic rights of others.

A less dramatic but still significant illustration of the tensions involved in this principle comes from teachers' strikes. Once the delivery system (i.e., the public school system) has been disrupted by a strike, certain alternative services are sometimes provided by the school board, by parents, or occasionally by the strikers themselves (who are often called "strikebreakers" for their actions). The alternative services usually center on graduating seniors and their admission into college. Classes are often set up so that they will have finished the required courses for college

on time. Counselors sometimes provide other services (e.g., helping to process college applications) to ensure that seniors will have
an equal chance of getting into the colleges of their choice.[23]

Students have a right to pursue a college education and,
especially in our credentials-minded society, to pursue it on
schedule. For striking teachers purposely to prevent that pursuit
would be an unjust intrusion on student rights. It would clearly
be a case of using harm to the students as a means of pursuing
their own goals.

I am convinced that teachers' unions would gain great advantages in a strike if they would set up these alternative services
themselves. They would thus make clear to parents, the public,
and the school board that their primary concern is for the students
and that they may be able to serve the needs of students better
than a school board that cannot prevent strikes and efficiently
manage its own system.

Other details in the experience of these examples could
change the ethical judgment about the situation completely. I think
it is accurate to conclude, however, that generally strikers have
no right to prevent clients from pursuing their rights by alternative
means or through alternative sources. On the other hand, strikers
do have the right to disrupt the ordinary delivery system, controlled by the management and owners with whom they are in
conflict, and to take measures to prevent them from providing the
service (especially by hiring new employees who would simply
take the places of the strikers) as though a strike were not in
progress.

Principle 8

**Human service strikes are unethical when they risk caus-
ing harm to clients and/or to the delivery system that is not
proportionate to the good effects which the strikes
reasonably intend to achieve.**

Practically speaking, this principle leads to two summary
statements that are derived from the actual outcomes of human
service strikes in the past two decades:

A. **Human service strikes are almost always unethical
    when they risk causing serious or irreparable harm
    to clients and/or to the delivery system.**

B. Human service strikes are often ethical when they risk causing only inconveniencing harm to clients and/or to the delivery system.

I begin the explanation of this principle by recalling a simple but often forgotten dimension of the process of making ethical judgments. *All* ethical judgments are made *before* the action is performed. Moral responsibility is greatest at the very moment that a person makes the moral judgment. It is not the actual effects of our actions that determine their morality. If that were the case, then no one would be responsible for moral decisions until days or weeks after the decision. If a person made dreadful moral judgments but, through chance, no bad effects followed, then that person could feel justified despite poor judgment and evil intentions.

Since all ethical decisions are made before the action is performed, then to speak about "risking" harm to clients is appropriate and most accurate. No one is certain about exactly what will happen during a strike. Experience and clear thinking, however, can give one a reasonable notion of what might happen. Thus, in trying to clarify the meaning of this principle, I will weigh the harmful effects a strike ordinarily could produce against the goals strikers may reasonably expect to achieve.

The key judgment to be made under this principle is the judgment about "proportionality."[24] Are the good effects that are likely to come from the action sufficiently grave to justify risking that some temporary harm may come from the same action?

Some might immediately object and maintain that, if there is even a chance of some temporary harm to others, one should not perform the action; it is against ideal Christian love to take any risks at all with others' welfare. Such a position, as pointed out at the start of this chapter, would be so rigid as to prevent a person from acting at all in many, if not all, tense situations. Life is so complex and the effects of our actions so interconnected with scores of other forces that even our best actions sometimes cause harm to some people. Human life would have to come to a halt if the basic presupposition for deciding about actions was "never cause any harm."

Also, the discussion of self-love in Chapter Four pointed out that the needs of everyone in the human community, including one's own needs, are to be treated with equal concern, and that inevitably some conflicts will arise in trying to decide which needs are more immediate and should be attended to in one's present actions. To choose one person's needs over another's will almost always cause some pain, but the best one can do in the human condition is to make the choice with a view to causing as little harm as possible and bringing about the overall welfare as fully as possible.

Proportionality, therefore, is *the* most important (but not the *only*) judgment to be made within this principle. One must attempt to determine, from past experience and from a sound analysis of the available data, the likelihood that some important benefits will come from one's action, as well as the probability that only some temporary harm will result.

The question of serious or irreparable harm

From the past experience of human service strikes, and from an analysis of the available data and of the feelings expressed by many involved in such strikes, I have concluded (in Summary Statement A) that the risk of serious or irreparable harm to others' welfare is almost always too great to take, no matter what benefits may come from the strike.

My reasoning for this conclusion is as follows. Most issues for which a union is pressing during a strike are ongoing ones that are part of the continuing struggle of life, e.g., better working conditions, fairer wages, and more effective ways of delivering the service. These issues are of real importance but are not of the "once-and-for-all" importance that a trip to an emergency room might be for a person in need. It seems disproportionate to weigh better working conditions for human service workers against the risk of patients incurring permanent physical disabilities because of the lack of necessary medical treatment.

This disproportion is obvious in some police and firefighters' strikes. The potential harm to citizens, if the unions have not planned in advance to have substantial alternative service, could be very serious, perhaps irreparable. The danger of criminal attacks that could cause serious injury or death rises sharply during a strike. The possibility of major theft or loss of one's home through fire also constitutes serious, perhaps irreparable, harm to innocent victims. Most issues at stake in such strikes do not seem to be as serious as the potential danger to citizens.

The phrase "almost always" has been carefully inserted in the summary statement. One could imagine, in an extreme case, conditions that might justify the risk of serious harm to citizens in a strike. Perhaps if the police department were largely controlled by organized crime, and the protection that the police were giving was already a threat to many citizens who were the opponents of the crime organization, a radical measure like a strike could be the only means available to challenge the untenable situation.

To their credit, police and firefighters' unions have generally recognized the great risks to the citizenry that their strikes cause and have been "in the forefront of lobbying efforts to require their government employers to submit to binding arbitration in the event of a bargaining impasse."[25]

Nursing home strikes (by professional personnel and not simply by support service personnel like cafeteria and maintenance workers) provide another clear application of proportionality. The kinds of harm that might result from such strikes are serious and very often irreparable. Besides the obvious danger to their physical health, the elderly clients might also suffer permanent disorientation because of the disruption of their stable life-style.

The potential harm to patients in nursing homes is a particularly sensitive issue for another reason, discussed in some detail in Chapter Five. Nursing home residents are among the most powerless people in our society. They have little control over their lives, and their need for help in even the simplest day-to-day activities is enormous. A growing insensitivity to the aged was epitomized in an extraordinary statement by Governor Richard D. Lamm of Colorado. He told a meeting of the Colorado Health Lawyers Association that elderly people "have a duty to die and get out of the way."[26] His subsequent attempts to soften the statement and deny its obvious implications do not hide the fact that he, and probably many other people in our society, believe that the elderly are living nonproductive, useless lives and should not necessarily have their rights respected.

Nursing home strikes not only endanger the physical and emotional well-being of the elderly, but they may be a subtle expression of this insensitivity to one of the most powerless and needy groups in our society. The ordinary issues involved in contract disputes are not at all proportionate to the kind of permanent harm that can so easily result from such strikes. The same conclusion can be drawn about strikes at residential institutions for the handicapped and the mentally ill. Residents in these institutions are extremely vulnerable to any disruption of services. The whole orientation of their lives depends on the stability of these institutions.

The phrase, "almost always," belongs in the summary statement, even when referring to nursing home strikes. One could imagine an extraordinary case in which a nursing home might be disregarding all sorts of regulations about ordinary care, allowing dreadfully unsanitary conditions, permitting gross understaffing to save money, etc. If a nursing home were getting away with such substandard care, a strike might be the only way to challenge the perpetrators to face the injustices. The potential harm to the clients from such a strike might be far less than the actual harm which they are suffering in the facility's substandard conditions.

Another example of a clear lack of proportionality between potentially serious harm and the possible benefits of a strike is the case of a strike at a hospital in a small population area. If no other health care facilities are within a reasonable distance and the local people have come to depend on this hospital for all their ordinary and emergency health care needs, then a strike at such a facility would threaten serious harm to these people. Even if emergency services were provided, the risk of harm to the residents would be significant because of the lack of alternative sources of health care. Such a strike would result in "an uneliminable, extra statistical likelihood of life-threatening situations arising."[27] The ordinary benefits to workers and even the benefits to the system pursued by the strikers would hardly be proportionate to the risk of harm to clients when no other reasonable access to health care is available.

The issue of powerlessness leads to the consideration of another example of a human service strike in which serious harm to clients, not ordinarily recognized, might render a strike unethical. A teachers' strike at an inner-city school might threaten serious, even irreparable harm, to students because of the special circumstances that surround many public and private schools in the ghetto sections of larger cities.

It is realistic to suggest that many minority students, who have been oppressed by the racist forces of our society since birth, have a much harder time "getting into the flow" of the educational experience than white students who have been supported by their upbringing to pursue education. The following scenario might be a reality at certain inner-city schools.

A significant number of students, for the first time in their academic careers, are getting interested in and seriously pursuing their studies. They are doing their assignments regularly, attending classes faithfully, and gaining a genuine respect for teachers and administrators. Some also depend on the school for a substantial part of their nutrition through government-funded breakfast and lunch programs. A strike would threaten to disrupt not only these values but might set off considerable vandalism in the neighborhood.[28] Such harm seems serious and could even be irreparable if many students, because of the nonsupportive environment in which they are trapped, never actually recover their positive spirit concerning education.

The issue of proportionality applies to the question of harm to the delivery system as well as harm to clients. If a private school or a small hospital in a large city were threatened with closing because of a strike, especially because of the strike's monetary demands, one would have to weigh the values and harm involved differently from the previous examples. What benefits could possibly come from risking the closing of a private school or small hospital? If such institutions were remaining in existence only because they were paying unjustly low wages to most of their workers, then it could be valuable for everyone involved to face that injustice and decide if they could correct it in order to remain in existence. It would be unreasonable to say that staying in existence is the ultimate value, no matter how the institution treats its workers.

If the union were challenging management about the way in which services were being delivered, the confrontation could also be valuable. In some small institutions, more resistance to change and modernization may exist than in larger institutions that have more interaction with contemporary methods and movements. Even if the future of the institution hung in the balance, a challenge to refurbish the delivery system could be healthful. One would be weighing a possible closing of an institution against the possible continuation of an inefficient or outdated system. As long as clients had access to the service through alternative sources, the risk of closing could justly be weighed against the efficiency and professionalism of the delivery system.

On the other hand, if the issue were primarily monetary and there clearly would always be limited resources for the private institution, then one could make a good argument for settling for wages a bit lower than other well-endowed institutions, as long as the wages were not unlivable.[29] Such a settlement could be ethical, especially if the small, private institution was very effective in delivering the services it promised.

Other instances in which serious or irreparable harm has resulted from strikes should at least be mentioned here. Teachers' strikes that have involved mentally retarded or emotionally disturbed children can and have caused serious, perhaps irreparable damage. Some evidence suggests that such students are quickly set back in their progress by sudden interruptions in their schooling.[30] Some never recover from these setbacks.

The erosion of relationships between teachers and students in a strike,[31] and the hostile relationships between nurses and administration after a strike,[32] can become permanent and affect the delivery of the service indefinitely. When such damage seems possible, service workers and management personnel both have a special responsibility to conduct themselves appropriately in those relationships so as to ward off the possibility of permanent damage. Threats, strident behavior, careless responses, and surly attitudes can be destructive to any relationship and must be avoided. Although everyone involved should treat the relationships with care, the workers have the specific responsibility to be sensitive to safeguarding the relationships, since they are the initiators of the strike (management initiates a lockout; workers initiate a strike).

The question of inconveniencing harm

Inconveniencing harm is real harm. It impedes and damages human growth and development. No one has a right to risk inflicting even inconveniencing harm on others as though it were a matter of no moral or ethical concern.

As we have stated several times, however, it is inevitable that all of us will sometimes do harm to others, even when our intentions are honest and unselfish. Some inconveniencing harm is part of the ordinary flow of life, part of the daily struggle of most human beings. Proportionality is therefore the key to determining if actions that seem certain to cause some inconveniencing harm are ethical or not.

When they enter into a strike, most human service workers are convinced that they have been experiencing some inconveniencing harm regularly in their lives. It is a real impediment to their human growth to be paid less than most other workers in the U.S. economy. It is damaging to their personal development to have no voice in determining how best to deliver their service. This lack of power is especially frustrating and dehumanizing, since it is they who have developed an expertise in the service and are more intimately in touch with the delivery of the service than their supervisors. By striking, workers risk causing some inconveniencing harm to clients and the system in order to eliminate other inconveniencing harm to themselves. The crucial point for deciding the morality of the strike is that they must not risk causing harm that is disproportionate to the amount of good they wish to achieve.

Teachers' strikes most often involve inconveniencing rather than irreparable or serious harm. Because of a strike, some students' plans to enroll in summer school may be disrupted if the strike lasts for an extended period. Vocational and college counseling for more advanced students, especially seniors, is usually interrupted. Strikes sometimes cause a hardship on families by requiring employment of baby-sitters or having a family member stay at home instead of going to work during the day. If a great number of school days have to be made up in the early summer because of a strike, students are set back in their attempt to find jobs for the summer.[33]

All these inconveniences are certainly harmful to students' smooth growth and development. If more serious harm is being done both to teachers and to the school system (and ultimately to the students) by the present order, however, then there could be just reason to risk such harm in order to improve the whole system. Extremely low wages (as has traditionally been the case in Mississippi[34]) can be very harmful to the teachers' dignity, can force qualified people out of the system, and can destroy the teachers' morale. To keep teachers powerless in terms of the major decisions that affect the shaping of education is not only harmful to teachers and students, but it also allows such decisions to become "political footballs," to be handled in terms of their value to the political careers of school board members.

Some evidence demonstrates that the harm caused by short interruptions in the educational process is not serious. A study made during an eight-week Pennsylvania school strike showed that no differences in scholastic achievement were apparent between students who had been in school and those who had been out during the entire strike.[35] The courts have frequently accepted the argument that, since the educational process is interrupted for many reasons as a matter of course, one can hardly make a case for a strike doing special damage to the process. "Schools are frequently closed because of communicable diseases, broken boilers, inclement weather, and a variety of other causes. The children may have an unexpected holiday but no one could seriously argue that there has been permanent damage and irreparable injury to their psyches, a deterioration of their character or irretrievable loss of their opportunity to learn."[36]

In nurses' strikes, when emergency and critical care services are usually well provided for, a different set of inconveniences appears. People must wait until the strike ends for their elective surgery and must rearrange the plans that they have made both at work and in their households. People with minor ailments who might otherwise have sought medical attention do not bother to do so, especially if they are poor people who do not perceive themselves as having other alternatives than the one city hospital clinic where they have always been treated with dignity. Putting off medical treatment in this way can lead to future complications in their health. The chances for mistakes in nursing care by temporary nursing personnel who are not familiar with the hospital or by supervisory personnel who are working 12 to 16 hours a day increase dramatically during a strike.[37]

The kinds of harm that nurses perceive themselves enduring are somewhat unique among human service workers for two reasons. First, the nursing profession has, to the present day, been made up almost totally of women. These women were expected to be subservient and nurturing and to find their identity in caring for others. Second, unlike most other groups of workers,

nurses had three dominant groups over them who have traditionally thought that they had the right to determine everything
about nurses' compensation, work-style, and place in the health
care community: boards of trustees, hospital administrators, and
physicians.[38]

Consequently, most of the early nurses' strikes were concerned primarily with changing the nurse's role in in the U.S.
health care system. Nurses wanted to obtain a voice in shaping
the health care system commensurate with their training and with
the fact that "many patients view nurses as more important to their
total recuperation process than their own attending physicians."[39]
Nurses' unions have considered this inferior role of the nurse to
be of greater harm to health care than the temporary inconveniencing harm caused by strikes (as long as emergency and critical
care services were adequately supplied).

One other example of inconveniencing harm can be seen
in strikes by support service personnel at hospitals, nursing homes,
institutions for the mentally ill, etc. When food service personnel, maintenance workers, or secretarial staff workers strike, the
institution is severely disrupted. The ethical considerations here
are rarely serious, however, since these services have only an indirect effect on the clients and are often supplied from alternative
sources, e.g., supervisory personnel and volunteers. To risk causing these inconveniences for the sake of fairer wages or more
appropriate working conditions could be just, as long as workers'
demands are reasonable.

What could become serious in such strikes would be direct
attempts to ensure that, e.g., patients would not have proper food
or that heating systems or electrical equipment would be
unrepaired and unsafe. These attempts would be direct attacks on
the rights of the clients and not simply disruptions of the delivery
system. It would be difficult to conceive that support service
workers could have grievances so severe that they would outweigh
patients' rights to proper nutrition, safety, etc.

Summary

It is impossible to avoid causing some harm in the complex
relationships of modern life. Even good actions will cause harm
to some people on occasion. The most important criterion for
judging the ethic of a service strike, therefore, is not: Will the strike

cause some harm to the clients? Rather, the basic ethical question must be: Do the hoped-for benefits of the strike outweigh any potential harm to the clients?

In evaluating the potential harm from a strike, everyone involved must understand that harm is not defined simply in physical terms of broken bones, sickness, or criminal attack. When dealing with human service strikes, much harm can be done to human relationships between workers and clients, between striking and nonstriking workers, and between workers and management. These relational values are often as important, and sometimes more important, than physical health and property values. To destroy relationships can be a very serious and perhaps permanent form of harm to everyone involved.

Finally, it is almost always unethical to risk causing serious or irreparable harm in human service strikes. The values being sought in a strike are simply not commensurate with such a risk. To risk causing some inconveniencing harm can often be ethical, since strikes ordinarily occur only when some inconveniencing harm already is being done, either to the workers or to the system (and consequently to the clients). Even when dealing with inconveniencing harm, however, one must be careful not to treat it lightly. It would be a sign of a dulled moral sensitivity to treat any human service strike as "standard operating procedure," as though the harm connected with it were simply an acceptable part of life that needed no moral scrutiny.

Notes

1. *Buffalo Board of Education v. Pisa*, 839 N.Y.S. 2d 938 (1976).
2. Samuel M. Gold, "Strikes by Public Workers," in R.E. Walsh, ed., *Sorry...No Government Today* (Boston: Beacon Press, 1969), p. 226.
3. David L. Colton and Edith E. Graber, *Enjoining Teacher Strikes: The Irreparable Harm Standard* (St. Louis: Center for the Study of Law and Education, Washington University, 1980), p. 31; Susan F. Appleton, *Appellate Review of Proceedings to Enjoin Teachers' Strikes* (St. Louis: Center for the Study of Law and Education, Washington University, 1980), pp. 23, 67; Edith E. Graber, *Michigan: The Warren Consolidated Schools Strike* (St. Louis: Center for the Study of Law and Education, Washington University, 1980), p. 18.
4. I am presuming that all the human services we are dealing, with in this study may be grouped under these three headings: (1) health care: a right to basic hospital care and nursing, to a physician's expert

care, to counseling, to mental health care in an institution if necessary; (2) education: a right to a regular school system, to special schools for the handicapped; and (3) public safety: a right to police protection, firefighting protection, public sanitation services, etc. A complete list of the human services considered here can be found at the end of Chapter Three.

5. John Finnis, *Natural Law and Natural Rights* (Oxford: Clarendon Press, 1980), p. 206.

6. William A. Galston, *Justice and the Human Good* (Chicago: University of Chicago Press, 1980), p. 127; Finnis, p. 200.

7. Finnis, pp. 198-201.

8. Wolfgang Huber, "Human Rights—A Concept and Its History," in Alois Mueller and Norbert Greinacher, eds., *The Church and the Rights of Man* (*Concilium* vol. 124) (New York: Seabury Press, 1979), p. 6.

9. Jan Milic Lochman, "Ideology or Theology of Human Rights," in Alois Mueller and Norbert Greinacher, eds., *The Church and the Rights of Man* (*Concilium* vol. 124) (New York: Seabury Press, 1979), pp. 15-16.

10. William N. Nelson, "Special Rights, General Rights and Social Justice," *Philosophy and Public Affairs* 3:4 (Summer 1974), p. 412.

11. Huber, pp. 7-9.

12. H.L.A. Hart, "Are There Any Natural Rights?" *Philosophical Review* 64:2 (April 1955), p. 183; Nelson, p. 411; Finnis, p. 199.

13. Richard A. McCormick, *Health and Medicine in the Catholic Tradition* (New York: Crossroad Publishing Co., 1984), p. 79.

14. See Robert Lanon White, *Right to Health: the Evolution of an Idea* (Iowa City: University of Iowa, Graduate Program in Hospital and Health Administration, 1971); John C. Hogan, *The Schools, the Courts and the Public Interest* (Lexington, MA: Lexington Books, 1974), pp. 1-4; Gaston Mialaret, ed., *The Child's Right to Education* (Paris: UNESCO, 1979), pp. 19-53.

15. M. Benjamin and J. Curtis, *Ethics in Nursing*, New York: Oxford University Press, 1981), p. 146.

16. See White, passim; Hogan, p. 4; Milaret, p. 19; McCormick, pp. 75-79.

17. Sanford A. Marcus, "Trade Unionism for Doctors," *New England Journal of Medicine* 311:23 (Dec. 6, 1984), p. 1510.

18. In the wording of this principle, it may seem that I am departing from a relationality-responsibility approach to morality and slipping back into a traditional approach, i.e., that it is *always wrong* to inflict direct harm on innocent people. The arguments in this section therefore will sound very much like arguments in the principle of double effect: that one may allow some harm to come indirectly from

one's action as long as it is not directly willed and as long as the good coming from one's action outweighs the evil coming from it.

Admittedly, my arguments in this section *appear to be* the same as those coming from these traditional sources, but, in fact, they are not based on traditional presuppositions. They are based on the two contemporary theological approaches I have consistently referred to in this book. First, my focus on "indirect harm" to clients in this principle comes from an *experiential approach* to moral theology. I speak of "indirect harm" to clients simply because this phrase best describes what happens in a strike. Workers withdraw their services. The act of striking does not include positive actions that directly harm clients. Strikers would have to make additional decisions to take such positive harmful actions as deciding to disrupt a college-board tutoring class or deciding to physically prevent volunteers from entering a nursing home. Striking is not an action that can of itself cause direct and immediate harm to anyone; it is an omission, not a commission. Thus the term "indirect" is used as a descriptive term and not for reasons of making a better theoretical argument about the morality of strikes.

Second, my arguments for Principle 6 are based on the *relation-ality-responsibility approach* to moral theology, but refined by a reflection on the "exceptionless norm" theory articulated by Richard McCormick, Donald Evans, and others. McCormick explains this theory as a form of contemporary proportionalism:

> It is a form of reasoning which frankly admits the existence of value-conflicts in our lives and goes about the business of attempting to discover which options deserve the preference in light of all the values, what is truly proportionate, what will enable us to wrest a maximum of good from the intran-sigence...of human dilemmas without slipping our grasp on the basic goods that define our possibilities for growth. (R.A. McCormick, "The New Medicine and Morality," Theology Digest 21:4 [Winter 1973], p. 320. See also R.A. McCormick, "Notes on Moral Theology," Theological Studies 36:1 [March 1975], pp. 97-100.)

Thus the "exceptionless norms" that McCormick and others articulate (e.g., no direct killing of innocent people, no killing of noncombatants in war) are not based on an absolute value of persons or actions. These norms are based on years of experiencing the consequences of the actions in question. If, after such experience, one feels confident that the actions have virtually always brought about more harm than good, and one has sound reasons for maintaining that they will continue to do so in the future, then one makes that exceptionless experience into a norm. If a rare exception has occasionally brought about more good than harm, one still concludes that given "human failure, inconstancy and frailty, and our uncertainty with regard to long-term effects," one should nonetheless hold to the norm as virtually exceptionless. (McCormick, "The New Medicine...," p. 320.)

In fashioning Principle 6, I maintain that *wanting to inflict direct harm on clients* will virtually always cause more harm than good in a human service strike. I have not found any situation where the circumstances of human service workers (or delivery systems) were so drastic that directly inflicted harm on clients would be a lesser evil than the continuation of those circumstances. I have not found situations in which directly inflicted harm (even directly inflicted inconveniencing harm) to the clients was so crucial to the force of the strike that the strike would have failed if the workers did not purposely ensure that the harm came about. Rather, the inconvenience to the owners and managers through the disruption of the delivery system seems to have always been sufficient to give the strike some real force. I attempt to prove these assertions through all the arguments and examples in this section.

Charles Curran maintains that there can be exceptions, even to "exceptionless norms." For example, a person might justly kill an innocent, randomly selected villager in a war if this action would save the lives of all the other villagers. (Charles E. Curran, *Themes in Fundamental Moral Theology* [Notre Dame, IN: University of Notre Dame Press, 1977], p. 125.) Perhaps Curran is correct in his reasoning about such an extraordinary and dramatic case.

I am arguing in this principle that there have not been and probably will not be such dramatic and extraordinary circumstances in labor relations in the area of human services. In other words, to justify service workers inflicting direct harm on their clients would require that they be in a dramatic condition of servitude or oppression that was so severe that they could not be liberated in any way other than by harming some of their clients. Such dramatic situations simply do not seem to exist. Thus, I write the principle in terms of the actual situation (since my entire approach to moral theology has been experiential), allowing that if dramatic and extraordinary situations were to occur, then this principle could be reevaluated.

19. Norman Daniels, "On the Picket Line: Are Doctors' Strikes Ethical?" *Hastings Center Report* 8:1 (February 1978), p. 29.

20. Cardinal John J. O'Connor of the Catholic Archdiocese of New York made it clear, in the midst of a city hospital strike, that the archdiocese would not approve of the hiring of any permanent replacements at Catholic hospitals affected by the strike, nor would they support such hiring at any other health care institution for the duration of the strike. See *The National Catholic Reporter* (Aug. 31, 1984).

21. Thelma M. Schorr, "Speaking of Ethical Behavior," *American Journal of Nursing* (March 1980), p. 421; see also Norman Metzger, Joseph Ferentino, and Kenneth Kruger, *When Health Care Employees Strike* (Rockville, MD: Aspen Systems Corp., 1984), p. 89.

22. "Three New Unions Strike as Yonkers Firemen Let Blazes Smolder," *The New York Times* (April 17, 1981), pp. A1, B2.

23. Colton and Graber, p. 36; see also Graber, p. 8.

24. Charles E. Curran, *Themes in Fundamental Moral Theology* (Notre Dame, IN: University of Notre Dame Press, 1977), p. 121; Bernard Haering, *Free and Faithful in Christ* (New York: Crossroad Publishing Co., 1981), vol. 3, p. 301; Austin Fagothey, *Right and Reason* (7th ed.) (St. Louis: The C.V. Mosby Co., 1981), pp. 427-428.

25. William D. Gentel and Martha L. Handman, *Police Strikes: Causes and Prevention* (Washington, DC: International Association of Chiefs of Police, Inc., 1979), p. 185.

26. "Gov. Lamm Asserts Elderly, If Very Ill, Have 'Duty to Die'," *The New York Times* (March 29, 1984), p. A16.

27. Daniels, p. 29.

28. See Colton and Graber, pp. 35-36, for an analysis of cases in which these kinds of harm were experienced. See also Appleton, p. 14.

29. See a story in the *National Catholic Reporter* (Dec. 21, 1984), "Out-of-work teacher says 'look at own house first'," for an interesting report of such a conflict at a private school in New York.

30. Colton and Graber, p. 42.

31. Graber, p. 23.

32. Metzger, Ferentino, and Kruger, p. 102.

33. Colton and Graber, pp. 35-36.

34. "Mississippi Teacher Walkouts...," *The New York Times* (March 7, 1985), p. A16.

35. Colton and Graber, p. 31.

36. David L. Colton, *State of Washington: Four Courts* (St. Louis: Center for the Study of Law in Education, Washington University, 1980), p. 44.

37. Metzger, Ferentino, and Kruger, p. 90.

38. Metzger, Ferentino, and Kruger, p. 98; see also Colman McCarthy, "The Nurses' New Voice," *The Washington Post* (July 22, 1984), p. K2.

39. Metzger, Ferentino, and Kruger, p. 90.

Part **III**

A Practical Evaluation

Chapter 7

The Value of Strikes— and Some Alternatives

The main burden of this book has been to formulate principles that will be helpful in determining the morality of strikes by workers who deal with the delivery of human services. I have suggested that the ethical dimensions of such strikes come primarily from four areas of evaluation: the duties of love and self-love, the sharing of power, the rights of clients, and the potential harm to clients and the delivery system. From a discussion of these four values, some strikes can be seen to be morally justified whereas others appear to be unethical.

This final chapter does not deal directly with the ethical dimensions of strikes, even though that has been this book's primary focus. Since I have adopted an experiential approach to moral theology and ethics, the book would seem to be incomplete without some discussion of the ultimate experiential question about human service strikes: What has been their practical value?

I ask this question with a view to answering a more specific question about the future role of strikes in collective bargaining in the human service areas. Are strikes of sufficient value that they should be considered to be an ordinary and accepted part of such bargaining?

Strikes have become an ordinary and accepted part of the collective bargaining process in industrial negotiations. Bernard Karsh affirms this fact with disarming clarity in a quotation previously mentioned in this book: "The strike is...the mechanism which produces that increment of pressure necessary to force agreement where differences are persistent and do not yield to persuasion or argument around the bargaining table.... Thus, the strike, or threat of strike, is the ultimate device whereby the competing interests of antagonistic parties are expediently resolved, leading to a *modus operandi* which permits both sides to accommodate their differences and live with one another."[1]

Strikes are an accepted part of the game in profit-making industries. If the statement just quoted truly represents the mentality of most people involved in industrial relations, then one could further say that strikes are a welcome part of the process. They help to keep everyone honest. They also provide a valuable dimension to labor-management relations that no other tactic could provide.

The question I am posing in this final chapter is whether or not such an assertion can be equally true in the collective bargaining process in the area of human service systems. Are strikes valuable? Do they provide a dimension that adds more than it detracts?

Obviously, any answer to this question is an opinion or, at best, an interpretation of data. I include my answer to the question here as a practical challenge to everyone involved in such strikes. Throughout my research process and interviews, certain practical issues continually arose from both sides of the controversy, issues that clearly led to a conclusion that such strikes are of very limited value even when they are ethical. Perhaps a discussion of these issues will be helpful—and, I hope, influential—in shaping attitudes for future relationships between management and workers.

Some problems specific to human service strikes

In Chapter Three I attempted to demonstrate that human service strikes are different from industrial strikes in that significantly different experiences emerge from work stoppages when clients are directly involved. As a result of these differences, certain problems arise that are peculiar to human service strikes. Industrial strikes have had little or no experience of them and consequently have had no solutions for them. I suggest that these are at least four specific problems connected with human service strikes that dilute their effectiveness and cast shadows on the benefits that they produce.

The first is that the pressure or force exerted by a human service strike is always limited by potential harm to the client. Human service workers cannot go "all out" in pursuing a work stoppage. If they would do so, they would probably cause serious harm to some clients, that almost everyone would call immoral. From a purely pragmatic point of view, they must "work against themselves," at least to some degree, when they strike. They must ensure that emergency cases are provided for, that the most powerless people in society are still served, etc.

Most industrial strikes do not have to face this complexity. There the fight between labor and management is more clearly defined. Owners and managers are directly pressured by the fact that they are making no profit on their investment. Consumers can go to other stores or companies to buy their goods. Indirect effects on other companies and other industries can occur, but these are not on *powerless clients* and consequently do not raise the kinds of tensions that are specific to human service strikes.

The limited data available about public opinion concerning human service strikes confirm that most people are highly ambivalent about their validity. On the question of teachers' strikes, "most polls reveal a remarkably even split between those who favor and those who oppose teachers' right to strike."[2]

No such ambivalence exists about the right of industrial workers to strike. This right has been affirmed and safeguarded in the U.S. law, at least since 1935 (the Wagner Act). This right is not questioned in any of the academic disciplines which treat the ethical dimensions of labor-management relations: philosophy, the social sciences, and theology.

In Chapter Six, I spoke of an ideal scenario for a human service strike in which management and workers confronted one another in an empty facility while all the clients went elsewhere to pursue fulfillment of their needs. Their human growth and development continued while management and labor struggled to resolve their differences. When the strike was over, the clients returned and the delivery system began to serve them once again. Of course, such a scenario is never realized. The disruption of a delivery system is always a complex reality. Clients, sometimes very powerless clients, are always caught in the middle of the confrontation; workers are always faced with the anguish of deciding how much service to render; and the public is always ambivalent in its evaluation of the event.

Second, a special problem arises about the unity of the workers during a strike that is rarely, if ever, a problem in an industrial strike. Human service workers, even when they have decided that a strike is just, reserve to themselves the judgment about how much service to render to needy clients. As professionals, they have developed personal relationships with their clients and often believe that they personally have the right to decide if the service will be essential to *these particular clients.*

When school counselors decide to continue sessions with certain troubled students or to offer their services to seniors preparing to enter college, they do not perceive themselves as "siding with management." They are simply making their own decisions about professional service based on their personal expertise. Some nurses will agree that the strike issues are just but that the needs of certain patients presently hospitalized are their personal responsibility. They refuse to go out on strike but do not criticize their colleagues who do.

Thus solidarity during a strike is a special problem for human service workers. Rarely do human service strikes evoke 100 percent participation from the workers.[3] This fact should not be surprising; the presence of clients brings a complexity to human service strikes that does not exist in industrial strikes. Steel workers or automobile workers could hardly say that they were returning to work to serve the needs of consumers who require their services. Nurses, teachers, police, and firefighters can state such a position with conviction. Consequently, the solidarity that exists in most industrial strikes will probably never be a fact in human service strikes. The ensuing bad feelings that often result between strikers and nonstrikers in human service strikes weaken both the union and the potential force of future strikes.[4]

Third, human service strikes have led to some erosion of worker-client relationships.[5] Such erosion does not mean that the strikers were acting unethically. It is simply an unfortunate fact that occurs because of the unavoidable involvement of clients in the job action. It is a further complexity that has no parallel in industrial strikes.

Lest I seem to contradict anything that I said about the justness of many service strikes in the preceding three chapters, I want to make clear that my only point here is to report and describe an unfortunate reality. Human relationships are delicate. The feelings of people who depend on others, especially people who are powerless, are particularly fragile. It is extremely difficult to withdraw services in such a way that all clients understand and *feel* that they are not the targets of the confrontation.

Patients who express feelings of "abandonment" when a strike takes place,[6] or students who carry signs with "Fire my teacher" printed on them,[7] may be expressing inappropriate feelings; they may be dealing unfairly with people who genuinely care about them. Such feelings, however, are an unfortunate fact in human service strikes that industrial workers do not have to deal with when they strike. This unfortunate reality weakens the force of striking for service workers, since it blurs people's vision concerning the real reasons for the confrontation and often puts the workers in an unfavorable light, even in a strike that is just on all counts.

The fourth specific problem is more subtle than the others, but nonetheless very real. Human service strikes work best against management personnel who are very conscientious and concerned about their clients. Strikes exert the most pressure against well-intentioned owners and managers and are least effective against management personnel who are not particularly concerned about clients.

From the interviews I conducted, I found that in certain school strikes workers complained of management not caring about how long the strike lasted. The workers contended that school board members were much more concerned about their own political positions, creating a "tough" facade in the community, and "teaching the unions a lesson." According to the workers, what happened to the students in the process was not the board members' primary concern. The pressure of a strike, therefore, varied in proportion to the concern of the school board for the students' educational welfare and for the effectiveness of the delivery system.

Health care employees and some union officials made similar accusations about management in the profit-making corporations, which have taken over about 15 percent of the hospital services in the United States in the past two decades.[8] They asserted that the corporations *wanted* them to strike. They perceived that the corporations saw themselves as strong enough to "win" any strike, and to make the unions look bad to the public (especially since the corporations have ample funds for public relations). The employees accused the for-profit corporations of caring more about establishing a powerful position in the health care industry than about the needs of clients who would be caught in the tensions of a strike.

Whether or not these specific accusations are perfectly accurate, the logic of this fourth problem remains persuasive. Owners and management who are not primarily concerned about their clients' welfare will not be as pressured by strikes as owners and management who are altruistic in their motivation for being involved in human services. Human service strikes, therefore, have the unfortunate effect of pressuring least those who need pressure the most.

I am not suggesting that human service strikes have been completely ineffective. As I implied in the discussions of self-love and power, strikes have helped workers to become more responsibly assertive and have allowed workers to share in the power of shaping the delivery systems. Through power sharing, workers have a better sense of their self-worth and personal dignity. Finally, through the pressure tactic of a strike, all citizens have been challenged as a community to face the question of a priority of values. If a society says that it places great value on education and health care for everyone and that it values the unique role of the aged, is that same society willing to allow people who are involved in these areas to be among the lowest-paid and most professionally disregarded workers in the United States?

Human service strikes have brought many benefits to clients, workers, and the delivery systems. That assertion is not disputed here. The question being raised is simply: Do these benefits outweigh the complex problems and tensions just discussed? In ordinary language, are they "worth it"?

The conclusion that I am drawing here is that a strike is an ill-fitting method for obtaining justice in the area of human services. There are so many limitations on using it in an "all-out" fashion and so many complexities because of the human relationships involved, that it will always be a tentative and clumsy means for resolving problems between human service workers and management. Unlike profit-making industries, in which a strike can be a clear confrontation between labor and management, a human service strike will always be an ambiguous reality. For a healthy future for human service work, viable alternatives to striking must be discovered.

Finding alternatives—some psychological barriers

Human beings find different ways to solve problems when they are convinced of the *necessity* of doing so. Rarely do people expend great energy for finding new methodologies if they are consciously or unconsciously satisifed with the old methods. When people have settled into one fairly acceptable pattern of problem solving, they can easily say, "There is no other way." They often need to be *forced* to look for other solutions.

A conversation I had with a retired construction worker many years ago illustrates well this first psychological barrier to finding alternative ways to resolve problems. He was reminiscing about his days working on the building of the first "skyscrapers" in the early part of this century. "We had a rule of thumb," he said, "that there would be one serious accident to a worker per story of the building. Forty stories to a building? You were going to have 40 serious injuries, including some deaths." He explained that management considered the cost of providing more effective safety measures, building safer scaffolding, etc., to be prohibitive. It just was not feasible. They were sorry that the construction business had to be this way, but there was "no other way" to go about it.

What caused management to change dramatically from such a position? Workers organized into unions and challenged this inhuman presupposition that safety was too expensive. Unions forced management to reconsider; they forced them to find "another way." We find "other ways" to solve problems when it becomes *necessary* to do so, either because of personal conviction or because outside forces are pressuring us to do so. Perhaps as a society, we are at this juncture with regard to human service strikes. Some pressures are at work—public opinion, the complex problems just mentioned, changing attitudes in law—applying a certain force to unions and management to find other ways of resolving an impasse in the collective bargaining process. There are also indications of real conviction on the part of both management and labor that other ways must be found to resolve impasse situations. The recent self-study document of the AFL-CIO, *The Changing Situation of Workers and Their Unions*, is an excellent example of this conviction. The authors state: "Collective bargaining is not, and should not be, confined by any rigid and narrow formula; the bargaining process is shaped by the times, the circumstances and the interplay between particular employers and employees. It is the special responsibility of the individual unions . . . to make creative use of the collective bargaining concept and to adapt bargaining to these times and to the present circumstances."[9] Individual unions are encouraged to make creative use of collective bargaining and promote the interests of workers, using methods other than the traditional adversarial posture that the general public has associated with unionization.[10]

Because of the self-study's emphasis on mediation and arbitration rather than on striking, Albert Shanker, president of the American I .leration of Teachers and a member of the AFL-CIO committee that produced the document, commented, "I consider this a revolutionary document."[11] It is revolutionary to presume that there are "other ways" to face the difficult confrontations within the collective bargaining procedure, especially when one contrasts these recent union statements with a famous quotation from National Postal Union President Sidney A. Goodman in 1967: "There *is not, never has been, never will be* any substitute for the right of employees to withhold their labor as a method of advancing their interests" (emphasis added).[12]

Management in human service systems has shown some movement to get beyond the previous model of labor relations, which was often authoritarian and paternalistic (or maternalistic) on their part. The National Catholic Educational Association is presently sponsoring a study, in correspondence with unions representing faculty at Catholic schools, on "Common Collaborative Models" for use by administrators and union leaders as they work out their relationships in the parochial school system.[13] Management consultants have suggested alternative models for carrying out collective bargaining and facing impasse situations. These models are explained in detail in the final section of this chapter.[14]

Robert Coulson, president of the American Arbitration Association, gives a concise explanation of a second reason why it is psychologically so difficult to get beyond the strike mentality in our U.S. society: "In America, real men don't mediate....Our society seems committed to adversarial competition. The American public expects to win; to field a winning team; to overwhelm its enemies."[15]

I have suggested previously that a primary reason why U.S. society is so competitive and so committed to adversarial relationships is our basic acceptance of the capitalist spirit. Whatever the reason, the fact seems clear in our society. To mediate, to compromise, and to be understanding with people who are in a power relationship with us is often interpreted as weakness, as being too "soft."[16] The macho U.S. spirit (and most strategies for labor relations, political systems, etc., in the United States have been formulated by males) seems to say that the honorable way to resolve a dispute is to "fight it out."

Chief Justice of the U.S. Supreme Court, Warren E. Burger, makes this same point about the foolishness of our competitive spirit in reference to litigation. We have become the most litigious people in the world. We seem ready to take almost any dispute to court. From 1950 to 1981, the annual Court of Appeals filings climbed at a rate 16 times faster than our increase in population! In so doing, we waste an enormous amount of energy and talent that could be used for much more creative human purposes. With many of the great masters of jurisprudence of the past, Justice Burger concludes: "There must be a better way."[17]

In order to leap over this psychological barrier to finding a better way to deal with conflict in the area of human service labor relations, perhaps we must become convinced as a society that a competitive spirit is not the ultimate measure of human strength. This spirit does not allow us to use our talents and energies most efficiently and creatively in the collective bargaining process. Indeed, "there must be a better way."

A third psychological barrier to finding alternative ways to deal with impasse situations in collective bargaining is based on a simple historical fact. In the history of unionization in the United States, many union leaders have developed great skills in adversarial collective bargaining. The strike threat has been an essential part of that bargaining process. To suggest that labor relations experts find alternatives to striking is to imply that some of those previous skills, developed through years of pain and struggle, must be considered out-of-date.

No one wants to hear that his or her hard-won expertise is no longer useful and is no longer the skill needed to face present and future problems. Everyone involved in collective bargaining in the human service areas must face that possibility. If it is agreed that striking is an ill-fitting way to resolve disputes in human services, then the collective bargaining process must change radically. Bargainers must come to the table with new and different skills that will fit more accurately the tensions involved in human service labor relations.

An alternative: compulsory binding arbitration

Compulsory binding arbitration is one alternative to striking that already has a history in labor-management relations. Conventional binding arbitration (sometimes called "conventional interest arbitration") means that union and management agree that a certain individual or panel of individuals will have final authority to set the terms of the contract that they (union and management) have been unable to negotiate. The arbitrator(s) makes the final decisions, usually in terms of a compromise between the positions of the two conflicting parties.[18]

A form of binding arbitration that seems to be growing in popularity today is *final-offer arbitration* (also called last-offer, best-offer, or final-position arbitration). In this case, the arbitrator reviews the final offers made by the conflicting parties and must choose either one or the other. The arbitrator may make no adjustment in any of the terms of the offers and may only decide which offer seems more reasonable. Depending on the prior agreement, the arbitrator chooses either the whole package or chooses item-by-item the more reasonable offer.[19]

Final-offer arbitration attempts to motivate both parties to develop more honest and reasonable positions before the arbitrator intervenes. "In theory, the parties, in an effort to win the arbitrator's approval, should be so close together that they will either reach settlement on their own, or narrow the area of disagreement to such an extent that the arbitrator's award, no matter which package is chosen, will be a reasonable one."[20] Fear that the arbitrator will select the other party's offer should cause each party to be very realistic and to have a down-to-earth sense of what resources are available and what conditions everyone in the delivery system could accept.

Some states have laws mandating binding arbitration for impasse situations in the negotiation of contracts by public service workers in "crucial services" (Michigan, Iowa, and New Jersey were among the first to have such laws). Police and firefighters' unions have been in "the forefront of lobbying efforts to require their government employers to submit to binding arbitration in the event of a bargaining impasse."[21] Australia experimented with a national law that required all bargaining impasses in every industry to be submitted to compulsory binding arbitration.[22]

The response to compulsory binding arbitration has not been uniformly positive. Many bargainers in the 1960s, both union and management, were very critical of the method, especially for what they have called its "chilling effect." These critics maintained that both sides were less interested in the collective bargaining process when they knew from the start that someone else would probably make final determination on the issues. Former president of the American Federation of State, County and Municipal Employees (AFSCME) Jerry Wurf observed: "There is no freedom at the bargaining table on either side when the gun of compulsory arbitration is pointed at the heads of the negotiators."[23] A policy statement of AFSCME in 1966 is even more critical of binding arbitration:

> If both parties know that, ultimately, an outside party will be brought in to make a binding decision on such matters as wages and hours there is not only no pressure on the parties to reach an agreement but even a fear of making any change in their original bargaining positions, lest the final arbiter use this attempted compromise as a starting point for further compromise. Thus, positions become hardened, resistance to the other party's proposals is increased, and the whole "bargaining" process becomes a game that is played out until the whistle blows and the referee, in some mysterious fashion, determines and announces the final score.[24]

Teachers' unions and other public employees' unions made similar critical comments about binding arbitration in the 1960s and early 1970s. The main focus of their critique was the suspicion that neither side would want to come closer together in their talks, since they both presumed that the arbitrator's judgment would be a compromise between the two boundaries set by the conflicting parties.[25] Others criticized the method simply because "it is inconsistent with the concept of living in a free society. All employee organizations and virtually all employer groups oppose it. Labor relations professionals oppose it, as do most politicians."[26] Anything that impeded the full freedom either of unions or of management to handle their own affairs was considered to be intrusive on the U.S. spirit of free competition.

Labor-relations literature of the past decade, however, seems to indicate a change in attitude toward binding arbitration on the part of both unions and management.[27] The interviews I conducted confirmed this impression, although union personnel generally seemed more enthusiastic about the method than management personnel. Perhaps one reason for the change is the greater emphasis now on final-offer arbitration. As already explained, this method motivates both parties to come "toward the center," to a set of terms that an unbiased arbiter might easily view as reasonable and realistic.

The attitude toward compulsory binding arbitration also changed because, according to much recent data, such arbitration does not actually have the "chilling effect" on collective bargaining that many of the participants feared. A study of the effect of the compulsory arbitration statute for public employees in Iowa reveals that, in the reporting years of 1977-78, 1978-79, and 1979-80, less than 5 percent of the total collective bargaining agreements were settled by arbitration.[28] In 1981 in New York, where mandatory arbitration exists for police and firefighters, only 11 percent of police and firefighters' negotiation sessions went to arbitration.[29]

In a summary of available data on final-offer bargaining since 1973, one study notes that less than 12 percent of the collective bargaining sessions that were legally bound to arbitration actually had to use that impasse procedure. In more than 88 percent of the cases, the bargainers resolved the issues themselves.[30] All this data seem to indicate that the bargainers were not restrained from entering into genuine bargaining because an arbiter was "waiting in the wings" in case they failed to come to a resolution.

As an alternative to striking, compulsory binding arbitration has two special advantages, besides the obvious one of avoiding the tensions and disruptions of the strike process. The first advantage has to do with the way the parties involved use their time and energies. Instead of straining to outmaneuver their opponents, they must be intent on educating and persuading the arbiter of the reasonableness of their positions.[31] Instead of posturing and manipulating, the bargainers are more motivated to deal with the facts of the impasse, since they know that the arbiter will have access to all the facts of the situation and cannot be outmaneuvered. Consequently, their energies are directed more toward the reality of the conflict than to mere tactic.

Second, one can make a strong argument for the position that a compulsory binding arbitration law may lead to greater justice. The argument of John Rawls may be used to support this assertion.[32] According to Rawls, an "ignorance condition" is necessary to guarantee the fairest decisions among persons with conflicting interests. By an "ignorance condition," he means that one must make decisions without taking into account one's own prejudices and self-interest benefits that are not really for the good of everyone involved. In other words, fairness requires that persons discount "prejudicial interests" in solving conflict-of-interest situations.

For example, if a judge attempted to arbitrate a case fairly in which her nephew was one of the plaintiffs, this fact could not be one of the reasons for her decision in the case. The judge would have to discount her prejudicial interest in her nephew as she made her decision. The judge could do this in two ways: either withdraw from the case or make an extraordinary effort not to consider this person as a relative.[33]

The possibility of compulsory binding arbitration as the final step in a collective bargaining process can force the bargainers to put themselves in a position similar to that of the judge in the previous example. If either party bargains solely from the point of view of self-centered prejudicial interest, the other party will almost certainly reject the proposal, and they will have to call in another "judge." If both parties try their best to take into account all the real conditions of their situation and do not simply emphasize their own prejudicial interests, there is a good chance that they will come to a fair resolution.

Thus, if both sides accept to some degree an "ignorance condition" about their prejudicial interests and try to take a more objective view of the principles and realities involved in the negotiations, their sessions may lead to greater justice for all. Compulsory binding arbitration, especially final-offer arbitration, by eliminating the value of posturing, may motivate bargainers to accept such an "ignorance condition," i.e., to deal more objectively with the issues rather than focus solely on their own demands.

In summary, compulsory binding arbitration allows the bargainers to exercise a valuable influence on the final terms of the contract, even though they give up ultimate control of the contract. The manner in which they influence the results of the process, however, changes radically. Skills that emphasize posturing, manipulating, and fighting are no longer a top priority. Instead, the skills of persuading and educating "the other side" and the arbiter become primary.

A second alternative: integrative bargaining

A concept of "integrative bargaining" has emerged in the literature of labor relations in the past two decades. An interesting way to explain integrative bargaining is to contrast it to "distributive bargaining." This contrast was introduced by R.E. Walton and R.B. McKersie in their book, *A Behavioral Theory of Labor Negotiations* (1965), and has been used regularly since then by labor relations experts.

Bargaining is simply "the give-and-take that occurs when two or more interdependent parties experience a conflict of interest."[34] In distributive bargaining, the two bargaining parties view their relationship as one in which "an increase in benefit to one party necessarily means a comparable decrease in that benefit to the other party."[35] In integrative bargaining, the two bargaining parties view themselves as colleagues engaged "in joint problem solving...the critical problem is finding a way to maximize the benefit of both parties, to assure that the conflict does not have deleterious consequences for both."[36]

To give an accurate sense of the contrast between the two methods, one may legitimately (but not absolutely) identify distributive bargaining with competition and integrative bargaining with cooperation. The two approaches to conflict resolution may be summarized in the following four points, which have been distilled from several major treatises on the topic.[37]

1. In integrative bargaining, both parties are primarily concerned about how everyone involved in the conflict can benefit by the solutions proposed. In distributive bargaining, the bargainers' primary concern is that their own interests be safeguarded. One must give as little as possible while attempting to gain as much as possible through the process.

2. In integrative bargaining, full information about the issues is shared so that everyone involved can propose solutions that are realistic and true to the facts. In distributive bargaining, the parties try to gain as much information as possible from the other party while giving as little as possible, in order to strengthen one's own position. Bargaining is viewed as a tactic of "information-manipulation in which parties fake, bluff, and so forth in an attempt to create certain impressions"[38] without giving a complete and unbiased picture of the actual situation.

3. Since the parties in integrative bargaining view themselves as colleagues involved in problem solving, great value is placed on reasonableness. Since the parties in distributive bargaining view themselves as adversaries in a power struggle, great value is placed on "toughness."

4. In integrative bargaining, negotiations are considered to be an authentic dialogue that aims at describing accurately and facing directly a difficult conflict situation. In distributive bargaining, negotiations are considered to be a series of tactical maneuverings that aim at securing one's own goals.

All collective bargaining is undoubtedly a mixture of some distributive and some integrative bargaining. I think it would be accurate to conclude, however, that collective bargaining in the industrial arena has been more heavily distributive than it has been integrative. The responsibility for this fact does not lie with unions. Initially, the responsibility fell much more to management because of the unwillingness of the original "barons of industry" to share any power with their workers. It would be historically inaccurate to conclude that unions have preferred to bargain distributively as a matter of their own self-definition.

Although the responsibility for the predominance of distributive bargaining does not rest with industrial unions, the fact remains that most unions have "grown up with" and developed great skills in distributive bargaining. Most unions brought such a mentality with them when they organized human service workers. To adopt an integrative bargaining mentality would mean a major shift in style for most unions. I have already argued that it is a necessary change in style when organizing human service workers, so as not to damage the essence of the delivery of human services.

"Collective gaining" is one of the more successful forms of integrative bargaining that has been used in contract negotiations between human service workers and management. It was developed by Irving Goldaber, PhD, of the Miami-based Center for the Practice of Conflict Management. Collective gaining emphasizes that the bargainers, from the start of negotiations, honestly describe their goals and concerns with no exaggerations, posturing, or bluffs. The bargainers are encouraged to explain the basic reasons and emotions behind their positions.[39]

Both sides must give detailed information about all the crucial issues in the bargaining process. This information sharing is intended not only to allow both sides to consider the issues as realistically as possible, but also to develop a trust between them that will help them to work together to improve the human service system.

Collective gaining (or the "Win/Win Program," as Dr. Goldaber has dubbed it) was used by the Catholic school system in Pittsburgh in 1983 with encouraging results. Before then, contracts were usually signed with great strain in September, a few days before the start of a new school year. In 1983 the contract was settled and signed in April, after only about two months of meetings.[40]

Both sides were well pleased with the results. Diocesan superintendent of schools Father Hugh Lang commented that the process helped both sides to realize that the goal of developing a better Catholic school system "is betrayed at a bargaining table, where we lie and play games to take advantage of each other." Teachers' union president Frank DeCaria agreed that "we needed an outsider to help us see the light," that we should "stop beating each other over the head" and instead work together to improve the schools.[41]

The collective gaining process (and integrative bargaining in general) necessarily involves power sharing. If both parties view themselves as colleagues cooperating to solve common problems, they will naturally share valuable information to which they alone have access and will be honest and direct about their goals and needs. In so doing, they will have shared some "expert" and "legitimate" power with the other, which should make both more competent for the task of facing the issues and shaping solutions. Thus integrative bargaining "is the grandparent of all forms of participatory management," and it might well be the "starting point for the development of such processes as collective policy-making, collective goalsetting and ultimately collective responsibility."[42] Sponsors and managers of human service systems must be particularly aware that true integrative bargaining requires an honest sharing of some power.

A third alternative: combination approach

In a recent study of health care strikes, the authors propose a creative alternative to striking that includes some mediation, fact finding, and arbitration.[43] Although the authors intend this process for health care enterprises, there is no reason why it could not be used for impasse resolution in any human service area. Five steps are outlined in this process.

1. During the life of the present contract, the bargainers should meet regularly to identify issues that were unresolved in previous contracts, as well as new issues that have evolved since the last negotiations. Labor and management would engage in frequent dialogue, educating each other about their positions, potential problems in their relationship, and possible solutions to those problems.

2. When formal negotiations begin 90 days before the termination of the present contract, the first order of business should be to identify a mediator-arbitrator who is acceptable to both bargaining units. This person's role will be that of a traditional mediator with one major difference: if the negotiations reach an impasse, the mediator becomes the arbitrator who will have the power to make a binding resolution of the impasse. The mediator-arbitrator will *not* be present for the first month of negotiations.

3. The mediator-arbitrator joins the negotiations 60 days before the termination of the contract, after the bargainers have had the opportunity to identify their positions on the major issues.

4. If an agreement has not been reached by 15 days before the termination of the contract, a fact finder will be appointed. The fact finder's report will be made available to the bargainers within 10 days, i.e., five days before the contract terminates. The fact finder's report will be in the form of a proposed solution for each issue in the bargaining. Everyone will be aware that this report will be a third choice for the arbitrator to consider if the issues remain unresolved and must be submitted to binding arbitration.

5. If negotiations are at an impasse when the present contract expires, the mediator immediately becomes the binding arbiter. The arbiter will decide on a resolution for each issue from the three proposals that are available: the last best offer of both bargainers and the fact finder's proposal.

This proposed process seems to direct the bargainers' energies to a collaboration similar to that proposed in integrative bargaining. The fact that both sides are in frequent dialogue during the life of the contract would almost certainly create a feeling of realistically working together and sharing in the power of decision making for the delivery system.

The fact that mediation, fact finding, and arbitration are mandated in the process would seem to obviate the value of posturing and bluffing at any stage in the negotiations. Honesty and directness throughout the whole process would seem to be encouraged by the way that conflicts would have to be resolved. Even the mediator becoming the arbitrator would encourage a directness between the bargainers, since this person would have gained some insight into both the wisdom and the honesty of the bargainers before being in the position of making final choices for them.

Practical conclusions—to the future

The withering away of the strike in human service enterprises and its replacement with viable alternatives will come about only if all the participants are convinced that the strike is a clumsy and ambiguous means for resolving conflicts. Even though many strikes are ethically justified, as I have attempted to demonstrate according to the principles proposed in this book, they are often very impractical and counterproductive.

All the alternatives proposed in this chapter imply that sponsors and managers of human service delivery systems must be willing to share power in significant ways. They must become convinced that sharing power willingly is far more productive and useful behavior than sharing power because one is compelled to do so.

Perhaps colleges and universities are in a position to make a special contribution to shaping a new kind of collective bargaining, because they have traditionally had a committee system that allowed for some authentic sharing of power by faculty members. As pointed out previously, that power sharing was so real in some instances that the Supreme Court decided, in the now-famous Yeshiva case, that faculty members should be considered part of management and not employees.[44]

If strikes are to be avoided, some alternative method of impasse resolution that effects a genuine power sharing is absolutely necessary. Without such an alternative, the collective bargaining process would be rendered ineffective and management would be empowered with that kind of "legitimate power" that would allow them to act arbitrarily. A classic example of such arbitrary behavior occurred in March 1985. The administrator of the Veterans Administration (VA) in Washington, DC, Harry Walters, reversed a long-standing policy by announcing that certain issues, such as grievance procedures, would no longer be negotiable in contracts between the VA and the unions. John Claya, labor counsel for the American Nurses' Association (ANA), stated that this arbitrary action by the VA destroyed any semblance of meaningful collective bargaining between the ANA and the VA. "The VA's position literally guts unions' ability to represent an individual nurse in discipline or discharge situations.... A negotiated grievance procedure historically has been the cornerstone of a meaningful collective bargaining agreement."[45]

A sharing in "expert power," put to use as "integrative power," is the key to more fulfilling and productive relationships between management and workers in the area of human services. Final-offer binding arbitration, integrative bargaining, and the combination of mediation, fact finding, and arbitration all seem to offer a "better way" to resolve management-worker conflicts in human service enterprises than the strike.

It would be a happy moment if human service workers and management personnel would wake up some morning in the future to discover that they needed a book on the ethics of strikes only for historical reasons and not for their present functioning.

Notes

1. Bernard Karsh, *Diary of a Strike* (Urbana, IL: University of Illinois Press, 1958), p. 13.

2. *A Decade of Gallup Polls of Attitudes Toward Education* (Bloomington, IN: Phi Delta Kappa, 1978), p. 238.

3. For some interesting statistics on the participation in five police strikes in 1975-76, see William D. Gentel and Martha L. Handman, *Police Strikes: Causes and Prevention* (Washington, DC: International Association of Chiefs of Police, Inc., 1979), pp. 202-203. The data do not indicate that all the police personnel who remained at work did so for altruistic reasons; but neither does it indicate that such motivation was *not* part of their reason for staying on the job.

4. Gentel and Handman, p. 202; see also Norman Metzger, Joseph Ferentino, and Kenneth Kruger, *When Health Care Employees Strike* (Rockville, MD: Aspen Systems Corp., 1984), pp. 101-102.

5. Metzger, Ferentino, and Kruger, pp. 143-144.

6. Metzger, Ferentino, and Kruger, p. 91.

7. David Colton and Edith Graber, *Enjoining Teacher Strikes: The Irreparable Harm Standard* (St. Louis: Center for the Study of Law in

Education, Washington University, 1980), p. 31; Edith Graber, *Michigan: The Warren Consolidated Schools Strike* (St. Louis: Center for the Study of Law in Education, Washington University, 1908), p. 23.

8. Arnold S. Relman, "Investor-Owned Hospitals and Health-Care Costs," *The New England Journal of Medicine* 309:6 (Aug 11, 1983), p. 370.

9. AFL-CIO Committee on the Evolution of Work, *The Changing Situation of Workers and Their Unions* (AFL-CIO Department of Information, 1985), p. 19.

10. AFL-CIO Committee, p. 18.

11. "AFL-CIO, Conceding Some of Labor's Problems, Offers Some Solutions," *The New York Times* (Feb. 22, 1985), p. A10.

12. This remark was made by Mr. Goodman to the Federal Bar Association, Seminar on Collective Bargaining in Federal Service, Washington, DC, April 18, 1967, and is quoted in Murray B. Nesbitt, *Labor Relations in the Federal Government* (Washington, DC: Bureau of National Affairs, Inc., 1976), p. 375.

13. Richard M. Lawless, PhD, Vicar for Education in the Catholic Diocese of Syracuse, NY, chairs this committee, whose full title is "The Committee on Collaborative Models for Chief Administrators in Catholic Education."

14. See William C. Pendleton, "Dispute Resolution: Challenge to the Social Sciences," *National Forum* LXIII:4 (Fall 1983), pp. 22-24, for a fine summary of recent theories on Alternative Dispute Resolution (ADR).

15. Robert Coulson, "Arbitration: An International Wallflower," *National Forum* XLIII:4 (Fall 1983), p. 19.

16. Coulson, p. 18.

17. Warren E. Burger, "Conflict Resolution: Isn't There A Better Way?" *National Forum* LXIII:4 (Fall 1983), pp. 3-4.

18. Metzger, Ferentino, and Kruger, p. 146.

19. Metzger, Ferentino, and Kruger, pp. 147-148.

20. Metzger, Ferentino, and Kruger, p. 148.

21. Gentel and Handman, p. 185.

22. "Avoiding Major Strikes: the Australian Way," *U.S. News and World Report* (July 15, 1968), pp. 85-86.

23. "Management at the Bargaining Table," in R.E. Walsh, ed., *Sorry...No Government Today* (Boston: Beacon Press, 1969), p. 38.

24. "Policy Statement on Public Employee Unions: Rights and Responsibilities (adopted by International Executive Board AFSCME, AFL-CIO, July 26, 1966)," in R.E. Walsh, ed., *Sorry...No Government Today* (Boston: Beacon Press, 1969), p. 69.

25. Robert P. Griffin, "The Challenge of Public Employee Bargaining," and David Selden, "Needed: More Teacher," in R.E. Walsh, ed., *Sorry...No Government Today* (Boston: Beacon Press, 1969), pp. 114, 228.

26. Richard P. McLaughlin, "Public Employee Collective Bargaining," in R.E. Walsh, ed., *Sorry...No Government Today* (Boston: Beacon Press, 1969), p. 295.

27. Gentel and Handman, p. 185; Metzger, Ferentino, and Kruger, p. 144.

28. John E. Beamer, "Fact or Fiction Regarding Interest Arbitration: The Iowa Evidence," *Selected Proceedings of the 30th Annual Conference of the Association of Labor Relations Agencies* (Fort Washington, PA: Labor Relations Press, 1981), p. 50.

29. Harold Newman, "Interest Arbitration: Impressions of a PERB Chairman," *The Arbitration Journal* 37:4 (December 1982), p. 8.

30. Metzger, Ferentino, and Kruger, p. 153.

31. Clifford Scharman, "Interest Arbitration in the Private Sector," *The Arbitration Journal* 36:3 (September 1981), p. 20.

32. John Rawls, *A Theory of Justice* (Cambridge, MA: Harvard University Press, 1971), Chapter 3.

33. James P. Sterba, *The Demands of Justice* (Notre Dame, IN: University of Notre Dame Press, 1980), pp. 30-31.

34. Samuel Bacharach and Edward J. Lawler, *Power and Politics in Organizations* (San Francisco: Jossey-Bass Publishers, 1980), p. 108.

35. Bacharach and Lawler, p. 109.

36. Bacharach and Lawler, p. 110.

37. D.G. Pruitt and S.A. Lewis, "The Psychology of Integrative Bargaining," in D. Druckman, ed., *Negotiations* (Beverly Hills, CA: Sage Publishing Co., 1977); R.E. Walton and R.B. McKersie, *A Behavioral Theory of Labor Negotiations* (New York: McGraw-Hill, 1965); Bacharach and Lawler, pp. 106-127.

38. Bacharach and Lawler, p. 120.

39. This information comes from a set of papers that the Center for the Practice of Conflict Management provides for parties who have contracted with the Center to go through the collective gaining process.

40. "Teachers 'Feeling Good' after New Bargaining," *The National Catholic Reporter* (May 6, 1983), p. 4.

41. "Teachers 'Feeling Good...'," p. 4.

42. From an unpublished paper by John F. Kinsella, "Collective Bargaining in the Catholic School System" (April 21, 1977), as quoted in Edward Marciniak, *Ethical Guidelines For A Religious Institution Confronted By A Union* (Chicago, IL: Institute of Urban Life, 1984), p. 16.

43. For a full explanation of their suggestion, see Metzger, Ferentino, and Kruger, Chapter 5, especially pp. 155-156.

44. *National Labor Relations Board v. Yeshiva* (1980), no. 75-857.

45. "VA Moves to Deny RN Bargaining Rights," *The American Nurse* 17:3 (March 1985), p. 1.

Index